# GOD'S WORD FOR US THROUGH JEREMIAH

THIS BOOK IS THE PROPERTY OF

© 2010
Watch Tower Bible and Tract Society of Pennsylvania
All Rights Reserved

PUBLISHERS
Watchtower Bible and Tract Society of New York, Inc.
Brooklyn, New York, U.S.A.

2010 Printing

This publication is not for sale. It is provided as part of a worldwide Bible educational work supported by voluntary donations.

Unless otherwise indicated,
Scripture quotations are from the modern-language
*New World Translation of the Holy Scriptures—With References*

Photo Credits: ■ Pages 54-55: Jucal seal and Gedaliah seal: Gabi Laron/Institute of Archaeology/Hebrew University © Eilat Mazar ■ Page 163: Edom: Pictorial Archive (Near Eastern History) Est.

*God's Word for Us Through Jeremiah*
English (*jr*-E)

Made in the United States of America

# CONTENTS

| Chapter | Page |
|---|---|
| 1 "I Have Put My Words in Your Mouth" | 4 |
| 2 Serving in "the Final Part of the Days" | 14 |
| 3 "You Must Say to Them This Word" | 32 |
| 4 Guard Against a Treacherous Heart | 43 |
| 5 What Friends Will You Choose? | 54 |
| 6 "Obey, Please, the Voice of Jehovah" | 67 |
| 7 "I Will Saturate the Tired Soul" | 81 |
| 8 Will You "Keep Living," as Did Jeremiah? | 92 |
| 9 Avoid "Seeking Great Things for Yourself" | 103 |
| 10 Are You Daily Asking, "Where Is Jehovah?" | 114 |
| 11 "Shepherds in Agreement With My Heart" | 128 |
| 12 "Was Not That a Case of Knowing Me?" | 140 |
| 13 "Jehovah Has Done What He Had in Mind" | 154 |
| 14 You *Can* Benefit From the New Covenant | 168 |
| 15 "I Cannot Keep Silent" | 182 |

## CHAPTER ONE

# "I HAVE PUT MY WORDS IN YOUR MOUTH"

"THERE exists a friend sticking closer than a brother." (Prov. 18:24) Have you experienced the truth of those inspired words? You can trust what a real friend says. When he tells you something good or explains what he will do, you believe it. If he points out something needing adjustment, you likely accept it and act accordingly. He has proved over time that he has your interests at heart, even when offering you counsel. He wants you to succeed, and you want the same for him so that your friendship will last.

² In many respects, you find such friends in the men whom God used to write the books of the Bible. What you hear from them, you can believe. You are sure that what they say is for your good. The ancient Israelites should have felt that way about the "men [who] spoke from God as they were borne along by holy spirit." (2 Pet. 1:20, 21) The one whom God used to write the largest prophetic book was Jeremiah, who also wrote Lamentations and two other Bible books.

³ You may have noted, though, that some Bible readers tend to view Jeremiah's writings as 'not for them.' They may imagine that the books of Jeremiah and

---

1, 2. Why do you have confidence in what you read in the Bible?
3, 4. How do some people view the books of Jeremiah and Lamentations, but why is that a misconception? Illustrate.

*"I Have Put My Words in Your Mouth"*

Lamentations offer only dire warnings and grim predictions.* But is that a realistic view of Jeremiah and Lamentations?

⁴ Granted, what Jeremiah wrote presents frank assessments, yet you know that at times a friend also does that. Even Jesus spoke out when his friends, the apostles, displayed wrong attitudes; he plainly corrected them. (Mark 9:33-37) Nonetheless, Jesus' main message was positive, showing the way to gain God's approval and future happiness. (Matt. 5:3-10, 43-45) It is similar with Jeremiah's writings, which are part of "all Scripture" that is beneficial for "setting things straight." (2 Tim. 3:16) Jeremiah did clearly state God's view of those who claimed to serve Jehovah but who deserved to reap the consequences of their bad ways. Still, the books of Jeremiah and Lamentations contain a message of hope and show how our future can be blessed. Jeremiah included prophecies about how God's dealings would develop, and today we are directly involved in the fulfillment. Furthermore, you will find in those two books statements that are positive and encouraging.—*Read Jeremiah 31:13, 33; 33:10, 11; Lamentations 3:22, 23.*

⁵ Both our present happiness among God's people and our prospects for the future are linked to things that Jeremiah wrote. Our unified brotherhood is an example. His writings will help us to strengthen that brotherhood and to apply the apostle Paul's counsel: "Brothers, continue to rejoice, to be readjusted, to be comforted, to

---

\* A number of languages use the word "jeremiad," meaning "denunciatory complaint" or "angry tirade." *The Washington Post* newspaper described a film on ecological and climate change as an "inconvenient jeremiad."

5. How can we benefit from Jeremiah's writings?

think in agreement, to live peaceably; and the God of love and of peace will be with you." (2 Cor. 13:11) Jeremiah's writings also relate directly to the message we preach. While we tell others about the last days and warn of the approaching end of this system, our message is still positive, offering a basis for hope. Moreover, what Jeremiah wrote is very useful in practical ways. Our situation finds many parallels in his life and in his message. To appreciate that, consider the background and assignment of this exemplary prophet to whom God said: "Here I have put my words in your mouth." —Jer. 1:9.

⁶ A husband and wife awaiting the birth of a child think often about their future son (or daughter). What will he be like, and what will he do in life —his interests, career, and accomplishments? Your parents likely thought about those things. It must have been similar with Jeremiah's parents. However, his case was special. Why? The Creator of the universe was particularly interested in Jeremiah's life and activities.—*Read Jeremiah 1:5.*

⁷ Yes, before Jeremiah was born, God used His foreknowledge. He took special interest in a boy

---

6, 7. Why can we be sure that God was interested in Jeremiah, and into what situation was he born?

*"I Have Put My Words in Your Mouth"*

who would be born into a priestly family living north of Jerusalem. That was in the middle of the seventh century B.C.E., not a happy time in Judah because of the bad rulership of King Manasseh. (See page 19.) During much of his 55-year reign, Manasseh did what was bad in Jehovah's eyes. Thereafter, his son Amon followed a similar course. (2 Ki. 21:1-9, 19-26) A dramatic change came about with the next Judean king. Yes, King Josiah searched for Jehovah. By the 18th year of his reign, Josiah had cleansed the land of idolatry. That must have pleased Jeremiah's parents; it was during Josiah's reign that God commissioned their son.—2 Chron. 34:3-8.

*Why do you have reason to be interested in the books of Jeremiah and Lamentations?*

## GOD CHOOSES A SPOKESMAN

⁸ We do not know Jeremiah's age when God told him: "Prophet to the nations I made you." He might have been close to 25 years old, the age at which a priest could enter the first phase of his service. (Num. 8:24) In any event, Jeremiah responded: "Alas, O Sovereign Lord Jehovah! Here I actually do not know how to speak, for I am but a boy." (Jer. 1:6) He felt reluctant, perhaps thinking he was too young or unqualified for the serious responsibility and the public speaking required of a prophet.

⁹ Jeremiah was commissioned during the time when King Josiah was eliminating detestable false worship and promoting true worship. However much interaction

---

8. What was Jeremiah commissioned to be, and how did he react?
9, 10. Under what circumstances did Jeremiah take up his commission, but why, in time, did his assignment prove to be daunting?

there was between Jeremiah and Josiah, the climate was clearly favorable for a true prophet. Zephaniah and Nahum also served in Judah early in Josiah's rule.* Huldah the prophetess did too, but she foretold bad times ahead. And Jeremiah lived to experience them. (2 Ki. 22:14) In fact, at times, such friends as Ebed-melech and Baruch had to rescue Jeremiah from certain death or protect him from vengeful enemies.

¹⁰ How would you feel if God said that you were specially commissioned as a prophet to deliver a strong message? (*Read Jeremiah 1:10.*) Consider just one example of what Jeremiah had to declare. In 609 B.C.E., Babylonian forces were moving toward Jerusalem. King Zedekiah sought a favorable message from God through Jeremiah. But that is not what God had for that king.—*Read Jeremiah 21:4-7, 10.*

## A HUMAN LIKE US

¹¹ Imagine that we had to deliver scathing denunciations and judgments against wicked kings, corrupt priests, and false prophets. Jeremiah had to do so. But we have God's backing, and so did Jeremiah. (Jer. 1:7-9) God showed confidence in young Jeremiah, emboldening him with the words: "I have made you today a fortified city and an iron pillar and copper walls against all the land, toward the kings of Judah, toward her princes, toward her priests and toward the people of the land. And they will be certain to fight against you, but

---

\* Later in Jeremiah's prophetic career, other prophets were his contemporaries: Habakkuk, Obadiah, Daniel, and Ezekiel. Jeremiah had served some 40 years when calamity came to Jerusalem in 607 B.C.E., and he lived for over 20 years after that.

---

11. Why might Jeremiah have found it difficult yet reassuring to carry out his assignment?

*"I Have Put My Words in Your Mouth"*

they will not prevail against you, for 'I am with you,' is the utterance of Jehovah, 'to deliver you.' "—Jer. 1:18, 19.

¹² No one need think of Jeremiah as some incredibly formidable person. He was a human like us. Moreover, it is significant that though Jeremiah lived in another era, he faced situations similar to those we face. We interact with various types of people in our daily life and congregation activities, even as Jeremiah interacted with those around him. This all relates to what we might learn from Jeremiah, who, similar to the prophet Elijah, was "a man with feelings like ours." (Jas. 5:17) Consider some examples of what we can learn from Jeremiah.

¹³ Over the years, have you not had ups and downs? So did Jeremiah. On one occasion Pashhur, a prominent priest, assaulted Jeremiah and had him put in stocks. For hours, he was confined in a wooden frame that may have held his feet, hands, and neck, forcing him into a distorted posture. In addition to the pain, he must have had to endure ridicule heaped on him by opposers. Do you think that you could bear up under malicious ridicule, even physical mistreatment?—Jer. 20:1-4.

¹⁴ Given Jeremiah's situation, it is not surprising that he felt moved to say: "Cursed be the day on which I was born! . . . Why is it that I have come forth from the very womb in order to see hard work and grief and that my days should come to their end in mere shame?" (Jer. 20:14-18) Clearly, he knew what despair was. Have you ever felt so despondent that you doubted your worth, what you were accomplishing, or even whether there was much point in going on? All who have ever had

---

12. What are some reasons why we can identify with Jeremiah?
13, 14. Why may some Christians relate to Jeremiah's experience with Pashhur, as depicted on page 10?

such feelings can benefit from a better understanding of Jeremiah's experiences and of how things worked out for him.

*What impresses you about Jehovah's commissioning of Jeremiah? Why can you identify with Jeremiah?*

---

¹⁵ The expressions of despair that we read at Jeremiah 20:14-18 follow right after the prophet spoke about singing to Jehovah and praising him. (*Read Jeremiah 20:12, 13.*) In your case, have you at times noted rather quick changes in your emotions? You were very happy, and then your mood changed to one of discouragement. Likely all of us can profit from analyzing Jeremiah's experience. It is clear that he had normal human feelings, as do we. So we can probably benefit greatly from exam-

---

15. Why can we benefit from noting the changes in mood that Jeremiah experienced?

*"I Have Put My Words in Your Mouth"*

ining the actions and reactions of this man whom the Creator was able to use mightily as a spokesman. —2 Chron. 36:12, 21, 22; Ezra 1:1.

¹⁶ Another reason why some identify with Jeremiah relates to his marital status. What was it? God gave Jeremiah an unusual and perhaps challenging direction: Do not marry. (*Read Jeremiah 16:2.*) Why did Jehovah tell Jeremiah that, and how did it affect him? What is there in this account that might resonate with brothers and sisters who do not have a mate, whether by choice or because of circumstances? In fact, is there something in God's statement to Jeremiah that Witnesses who are now married should ponder? And what of married couples who do not have "sons and daughters"? How can the account of Jeremiah help you?

¹⁷ It is interesting that at one point Jeremiah urged the reigning Judean king: "Obey, please, the voice of Jehovah in what I am speaking to you, and it will go well with you, and your soul will continue to live." (Jer. 38:20) This account offers excellent guidance about our interaction with others. That includes dealings with people who are not yet walking in Jehovah's ways but whom we may be able to help. Also, Jeremiah's actions toward those who were obeying God is a practical pattern for us today. Yes, we can learn a great deal from Jeremiah.

## WHAT IS TO COME?

¹⁸ This volume will help you to examine the Bible

---

16. Jeremiah's marital status may be noteworthy to whom?
17. The prophet's words found at Jeremiah 38:20 may cause us to think of what?
18, 19. What are some ways in which the books of Jeremiah and Lamentations could be considered?

books of Jeremiah and Lamentations and to learn from them. How? Under inspiration, the apostle Paul wrote: "All Scripture is inspired of God and beneficial for teaching, for reproving, for setting things straight, for disciplining in righteousness." (2 Tim. 3:16) That includes the two books just mentioned.

[19] Of course, the books of Jeremiah and Lamentations could be approached beneficially in various ways. For instance, one might study those two books verse by verse, seeking to understand the background or import of each verse. Or one could concentrate on valid parallels—individuals and events described in Jeremiah and Lamentations set alongside or contrasted with modern equivalents or developments. (Compare Jeremiah 24: 6, 7; 1 Corinthians 3:6.) Another mode might be to

*"I Have Put My Words in Your Mouth"*

study the historical setting and events illuminated by these two books. (Jer. 39:1-9) In fact, to an extent, some of such information is necessary for any rewarding examination of Jeremiah and Lamentations. Thus, Chapter 2, "Serving in 'the Final Part of the Days,'" will help us to get an overview of what the historical period that Jeremiah lived through was like and how God's guiding hand came into play.

[20] But the main thrust of this volume is different. We will approach the books of Jeremiah and Lamentations as gifts from God to help us live as Christians today. (Titus 2:12) We will realize even more than ever that these two books contain abundant information that is "beneficial for teaching." They offer practical advice and examples that can enable us to be competent and equipped as we face life's challenges. That is the case whether we are single, married, elders, pioneers, breadwinners, housewives, or students at school. Each of us will discover in these two inspired books divine help to be "equipped for every good work."—2 Tim. 3:17.

[21] As you consider each chapter in this volume, look for points that you can use. There is no doubt that the books of Jeremiah and Lamentations will underscore what Paul wrote: "All the things that were written aforetime were written for our instruction, that through our endurance and through the comfort from the Scriptures we might have hope."—Rom. 15:4.

---

20. What approach to the books of Jeremiah and Lamentations will we take in this volume?
21. Why are you looking forward to the study program to follow?

*As respects your daily life, what might you learn from studying the books of Jeremiah and Lamentations?*

## CHAPTER TWO

# SERVING IN "THE FINAL PART OF THE DAYS"

"WHAT are you seeing?" God asked his newly commissioned prophet. "A widemouthed cooking pot blown upon is what I am seeing," answered young Jeremiah, "and its mouth is away from the north." That vision gave an early indication of the sort of declaration that Jeremiah would make. (*Read Jeremiah 1:13-16.*) The figurative cooking pot was being blown upon, not to cool

---

1, 2. (a) What vision did Jeremiah have that set the theme for his prophetic declarations? (b) Why should you be interested in Jeremiah's message?

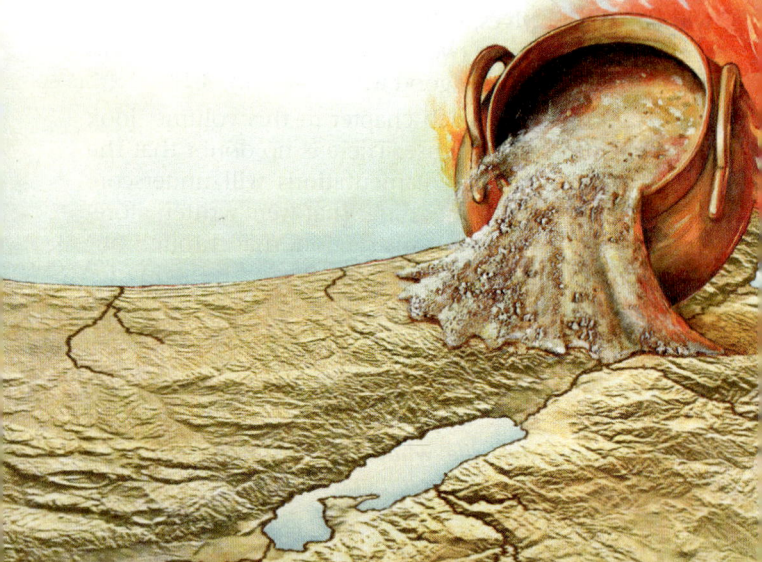

## Serving in "the Final Part of the Days"

it, but to intensify the flames underneath. Yes, Jehovah was foretelling that trouble, like a scalding liquid, would pour from this pot onto the land of Judah because of the prevailing unfaithfulness. Why do you think the pot's mouth was tilted southward? It meant that trouble would come from the north—Babylon would invade from that direction. And so it proved to be. During his years as a prophet, Jeremiah witnessed successive outpourings from this boiling cooking pot, culminating in the destruction of Jerusalem.

² Babylon is no more, but you have reason to be interested in Jeremiah's prophetic messages. Why? Because you live in "the final part of the days" when many claim that they are Christians; yet they and their churches do not have God's favor. (Jer. 23:20) In contrast, like Jeremiah, you and your fellow Witnesses are preaching a message not only of judgment but also of hope.

³ Jeremiah likely dictated his account to a secretary in the latter part of his prophetic career, rather than recording events as they happened. (Jer. 25:1-3; 36:1, 4, 32) The book is not in chronological order because Jeremiah arranged many parts of it according to subject. Thus, you should find it useful to get an overview of the historical backdrop of the books of Jeremiah and Lamentations and the order in which events occurred. Note the chart on page 19. Your knowing who was king of Judah at what point and, in some cases, what was going on in and around Judah will enable you to understand better what Jeremiah said or did. And you will be better prepared to benefit from God's messages for His people as proclaimed by Jeremiah.

---

3. (a) How is the material in the Bible book of Jeremiah arranged? (b) What is the objective of Chapter 2 of this volume?

## JEREMIAH IN HIS HISTORICAL SETTING

⁴ Jeremiah prophesied during a period of turbulent changes. It was a time of rivalry between Assyria, Babylon, and Egypt. Some 93 years before the start of Jeremiah's prophetic career, Assyria defeated the northern ten-tribe kingdom of Israel and deported many of its inhabitants. At that time, Jehovah defended Jerusalem and its faithful king, Hezekiah, against Assyrian assault. You will recall how God miraculously slew 185,000 enemy soldiers. (2 Ki. 19:32-36) One of Hezekiah's sons was Manasseh. Jeremiah was likely born during Manasseh's 55-year reign, a time when Judah came under Assyrian political control.—2 Chron. 33:10, 11.

⁵ Jeremiah wrote the books of 1 and 2 Kings, in which we read that Manasseh rebuilt the high places that his father had destroyed. Manasseh set up altars to Baal and to the army of the heavens, even in Jehovah's temple. And Manasseh spilled much innocent blood, having his own son offered as a burnt sacrifice to a false god. In sum, "he did on a large scale what was bad in Jehovah's eyes." Because of all that wickedness, God decreed that calamity would come upon Jerusalem and Judah, as it already had on Samaria and Israel. (2 Ki. 21:1-6, 12-16) After Manasseh's death, his son Amon continued his father's idolatrous practices, but soon things would change. After two years, Amon was murdered, and his eight-year-old son Josiah came to the throne in 659 B.C.E.

⁶ During Josiah's 31-year reign, Babylon began to gain the upper hand over Assyria. Josiah saw in this situation an opening to regain Judah's independence from foreign domination. Unlike his father and grandfather, Josiah

---

4-6. What was the situation of God's ancient people in the decades preceding Jeremiah's prophetic career?

served Jehovah faithfully and instituted major religious reforms. (2 Ki. 21:19–22:2) In his 12th year as king, Josiah destroyed the high places, the sacred poles, and the false religious images throughout his kingdom and thereafter ordered that Jehovah's temple be repaired. (*Read 2 Chronicles 34:1-8.*) Interestingly, it was in the 13th year of Josiah's reign (647 B.C.E.) that Jeremiah was commissioned as God's prophet.

*How might you have felt had you been a prophet in Jeremiah's day?*

---

⁷ While the temple was being restored, in the 18th year of good King Josiah's reign, the high priest found "the very book of the law." The king had his secretary read it to him. Josiah recognized the errors of his people, sought Jehovah's guidance through the prophetess Huldah, and urged his subjects to keep God's commandments. Huldah informed Josiah that Jehovah would bring "calamity" on the Judeans on account of their unfaithfulness. However, because of Josiah's good attitude toward pure worship, that calamity would not come during his lifetime.—2 Ki. 22:8, 14-20.

⁸ King Josiah renewed his efforts to eliminate all the trappings of idolatry. This drive even took him into territory once occupied by the northern kingdom of Israel, to pull down the high place and the altar at Bethel. He also arranged for an outstanding celebration of the Passover. (2 Ki. 23:4-25) Think how this must have pleased Jeremiah! It proved difficult, though, to move the people to

---

7, 8. (a) How did King Josiah's reign differ from those of his predecessors, Manasseh and Amon? (b) What kind of person was Josiah? (See the box on page 20.)

change their ways. Manasseh and Amon had introduced the people to degraded idol worship, so spirituality was at a low ebb. Despite Josiah's reforms, God moved Jeremiah to point out that the Judeans' gods were as many as their cities. The prophet's fellow countrymen were like an unfaithful wife—they had left Jehovah and prostituted themselves to foreign gods. Jeremiah declared: "As many altars as the streets of Jerusalem you people have placed for the shameful thing, altars to make sacrificial smoke to Baal."—*Read Jeremiah 11:1-3, 13.*

⁹ Just as Jeremiah's delivering of such messages did not change the Jews, so it did not alter the fact that surrounding nations were jostling to gain ascendancy. In 632 B.C.E., the combined forces of the Babylonians and the Medes conquered Nineveh, the Assyrian capital. Three years later, Pharaoh Necho of Egypt led his army north to assist the beleaguered Assyrians. For reasons not stated in the Bible, Josiah tried to turn the Egyptian forces back at Megiddo, but he was mortally wounded. (2 Chron. 35:20-24) What political and religious changes would this sad event bring to Judah? And what new challenges would Jeremiah face?

## A CHANGE OF RELIGIOUS CLIMATE

¹⁰ Imagine how Jeremiah must have felt on learning of Josiah's death! Moved with grief, he chanted dirges over the king. (2 Chron. 35:25) This was already a time of worry, and international instability brought pressure on Judah. The rival powers—Egypt, Assyria, and Bab-

---

9. The last years of Josiah's reign were marked by what international events?
10. (a) In what sense were the times following Josiah's death similar to our times? (b) How can you benefit from examining Jeremiah's conduct?

ylon—were jockeying for control of the region. And the religious climate within Judah had changed with Josiah's death. That was the end of a regime essentially favorable toward Jeremiah's activity and the beginning of a hostile one. Many of our brothers in modern times have experienced a similar change, from relative freedom of worship to persecutions and bans. Who knows how many of us might soon experience similar changes? How might that affect us? What might we have to do to maintain our integrity? With those questions in mind, it will be encouraging to note the challenges that Jeremiah met successfully.

¹¹ The inhabitants of Judah put Josiah's son Jehoahaz on the throne in Jerusalem. Jehoahaz, also known as Shallum, reigned for just three months. When Pharaoh Necho returned south after fighting the Babylonians, he removed the new king and took him to

---

11. What developed in Judah after the death of Josiah?

### Jeremiah's Service

- Manasseh
- Amon 661 — 660 B.C.E.
- Josiah 659 — 650
- **Jeremiah commissioned c. 647** — 640
- Nineveh destroyed 632 — 630
- Jehoahaz 628 (three months)
- Jehoiakim 628 — 620
- Jehoiachin 618 (three months)
- Zedekiah 617 — 610
- Jerusalem destroyed 607 — 600, 590, 580

## JOSIAH—THE LAST OF JUDAH'S GOOD KINGS

Upon the death of his father, Amon, Josiah became king of Judah at age eight. When he was 15, he began to search for God and "to walk in all the way of David his forefather." When he was 19, he began to cleanse Judah and Israel of their places of false worship and to smash their idols. At age 25, he began to have Jehovah's temple repaired.—2 Ki. 21:19–22:2; 2 Chron. 34:2-8.

The book of the Law, likely the original written by Moses, was found during the temple restoration and was read to Josiah. He humbled himself, tore his garments, and wept. Josiah arranged for the priests, the Levites, and all his subjects, the great and the small, to hear the reading of the book. The king concluded a covenant, says the account, "to go following Jehovah and to keep his commandments . . . with all his heart and with all his soul." Thereafter, Josiah undertook a more extensive campaign to eliminate false worship. The king also held a great Passover to Jehovah, the like of which had not been seen since the days of Samuel.—2 Chron. 34:14–35:19.

Egypt, and Jeremiah declared that Jehoahaz would "return no more." (Jer. 22:10-12; 2 Chron. 36:1-4) In his place, Necho enthroned Jehoiakim, another of Josiah's sons. Jehoiakim did not imitate his father's good example. Far from continuing his father's reforms, he practiced idolatry.—*Read 2 Kings 23:36, 37.*

¹² At the start of Jehoiakim's reign, Jehovah told Jeremiah to go to the temple and roundly condemn the Judeans for their wickedness. They considered Jehovah's temple to be a talisman that would protect them. Yet, if they would not abandon their "stealing, murdering and committing adultery and swearing falsely and making sacrificial smoke to Baal and walking after other gods," Jehovah would forsake his temple. And he would do the same to the hypocrites who worshipped in it, just as he abandoned the tabernacle at Shiloh in the days of High Priest Eli. The land of Judah would "become nothing but a devastated place." (Jer. 7:1-15, 34; 26:1-6)\* Think of the courage Jeremiah needed to declare that message! Likely, he did so in public before prominent, influential people. Some brothers and sisters today have likewise felt that they needed a measure of courage to share in street witnessing or to address wealthy or important people. We can, though, be sure of this: God's support for us is certain, just as it was for Jeremiah.—Heb. 10:39; 13:6.

¹³ Given the religious and political climate prevailing in Judah, how would the religious leaders react to Jeremiah's speech? According to the prophet's own

---

\* The similarity between Jeremiah 7:1-15 and 26:1-6 has led some to conclude that both passages refer to the same event.

---

12, 13. (a) At the start of Jehoiakim's reign, what religious climate prevailed? (b) How did the Jewish religious leaders treat Jeremiah?

account, "the priests and the prophets and all the people laid hold of [me], saying: 'You will positively die.'" They were livid, declaring: "To this man the judgment of death belongs." (*Read Jeremiah 26:8-11.*) Jeremiah's opponents, however, did not prevail. Jehovah was with his prophet to deliver him. As for Jeremiah personally, he did not allow the opponents' menacing appearance or numbers to frighten him. Neither should you.

*How would you contrast conditions during the reigns of Manasseh, Amon, and Josiah? What lesson might you find in how Jeremiah faced his challenging assignment?*

*Serving in "the Final Part of the Days"*

## "YOU MUST WRITE . . . ALL THE WORDS"

¹⁴ In the fourth year of the reign of Jehoiakim, Jehovah told Jeremiah to write down all the words that Jehovah had spoken to him since the days of Josiah. Jeremiah thus dictated to his secretary, Baruch, all that God had told him in the preceding 23 years. His messages of judgment involved some 20 kings and kingdoms. Jeremiah commanded Baruch to read this scroll aloud in Jehovah's house. The objective of this effort? "Perhaps those of the house of Judah will listen to all the calamity that I am thinking of doing to them," said Jehovah, "to the end that they may return, each one from his bad way, and that I may actually forgive their error and their sin."—Jer. 25:1-3; 36:1-3.

¹⁵ When a court official read the scroll to Jehoiakim, the king cut it up and burned it. He then ordered that Jeremiah and Baruch be brought before him. "But Jehovah kept them concealed." (*Read Jeremiah 36:21-26.*) Because of Jehoiakim's thoroughly bad attitude, Jehovah, through his prophet, declared that the king would have "the burial of a he-ass." He would be 'dragged about and thrown away, out beyond the gates of Jerusalem.' (Jer. 22:13-19) Do you think that this graphic prophecy could be dismissed as an exaggeration on Jeremiah's part?

¹⁶ Despite having to deliver such messages of judgment, Jeremiah was not a prophet of doom. He also announced a message of hope. Jehovah would deliver a remnant of Israel from their enemies and restore them

---

14, 15. (a) What work did Jeremiah and his secretary, Baruch, begin in the fourth year of Jehoiakim's reign? (b) What kind of person was Jehoiakim? (See the box on page 25.)
16. Jeremiah proclaimed what positive message?

to their own land, where they would dwell in security. God would establish "a new" and "indefinitely lasting covenant" with his people and write his law in their heart. He would forgive their errors and remember their sins no more. Moreover, a descendant of David would "execute justice and righteousness in the land." (Jer. 31: 7-9; 32:37-41; 33:15) These prophecies were to have their fulfillment in the decades and centuries to come, even a fulfillment that touches our lives and can brighten our everlasting future. But back in Jeremiah's day, Judah's enemies continued their maneuvers.—*Read Jeremiah 31: 31, 33, 34; Hebrews 8:7-9; 10:14-18.*

## THE RISE OF BABYLON

[17] In 625 B.C.E., the Babylonians and Egyptians fought a decisive battle at Carchemish, near the Euphrates River some 370 miles north of Jerusalem. King Nebuchadnezzar vanquished Pharaoh Necho's forces, ending Egyptian power in the region. (Jer. 46:2) Nebuchadnezzar now dominated Judah, and Jehoiakim was forced to be his servant. After three years of vassalage, however, Jehoiakim rebelled. (2 Ki. 24:1, 2) In response, Nebuchadnezzar and his army marched into Judah in 618 B.C.E. and surrounded Jerusalem. Try to picture how turbulent a time that was, even for God's prophet Jeremiah. Jehoiakim apparently met his end during the siege.* His son Jehoiachin

---

* Daniel 1:1, 2 says that Jehoiakim was given into Nebuchadnezzar's hand in Jehoiakim's third year, apparently of his vassalage. This may mean that the king died during the siege, which ultimately succeeded. There is no Biblical confirmation of Josephus' report that Nebuchadnezzar killed Jehoiakim and had his body thrown outside Jerusalem's walls without a burial.—Jer. 22:18, 19; 36:30.

---

17, 18. What international events marked the last years of Jehoiakim's reign and that of Zedekiah?

## JEHOIAKIM —THE KING WHO KILLED JEHOVAH'S PROPHET

Jehoiakim was 25 years old when he came to the throne of Judah, and he reigned about 11 years. The summary of his acts recorded at 2 Chronicles 36:5-8 notes that he did, not just bad, but "detestable things." Ignoring Jeremiah's warnings, Jehoiakim ruled by injustice, extortion, and murder. When Urijah the prophet spoke a message similar to Jeremiah's, Jehoiakim had him murdered. It appears that the king himself died during the Babylonian siege of Jerusalem.—Jer. 22:17-19; 26:20-23.

surrendered to the Babylonians after occupying Judah's throne for just three months. Nebuchadnezzar stripped Jerusalem of its riches and took into exile Jehoiachin, the families of the king and of the nobles of Judah, the nation's mighty men, and its craftsmen. Among the exiles were Daniel, Hananiah, Mishael, and Azariah.—2 Ki. 24:10-16; Dan. 1:1-7.

<sup>18</sup> Nebuchadnezzar now made Zedekiah, another of Josiah's sons, king of Judah. He was to be the last earthly

king of the Davidic line. His reign ended when Jerusalem and its temple were destroyed in 607 B.C.E. (2 Ki. 24:17) The 11 years of Zedekiah's reign, though, were marked by great social and political tensions in Judah. Clearly, Jeremiah had to trust implicitly in the One who had commissioned him as a prophet.

[19] Put yourself in Jeremiah's place. Since Josiah's time, Jeremiah had seen political upheaval and spiritual deterioration among God's people. However, he knew that things would get worse. The people of his hometown told him: "You must not prophesy in the name of Jehovah, that you may not die at our hand." (Jer. 11:21) Even when Jeremiah's prophecies came true, the Jews said: "As regards the word that you have spoken to us in the name of Jehovah, we are not listening to you." (Jer. 44:16) Yet, people's lives were at stake, just as they are today. The message you proclaim is from Jehovah, just as Jeremiah's was. That being the case, you can fortify your zeal for the ministry by examining how Jehovah protected his prophet during the period leading up to Jerusalem's fall.

---

19. How did Jeremiah's contemporaries react to his message, and why should that interest you?

*What can we learn from Jeremiah's attitude during Jehoiakim's reign? Jeremiah pronounced what outstanding prophecy that reaches our time?*

## THE CLOSING DAYS OF A DYNASTY

[20] Perhaps the hardest years of Jeremiah's prophetic career were during Zedekiah's reign. Like many of his

---

20. Why was Zedekiah's reign particularly difficult for Jeremiah? (See the box on page 29.)

## Serving in "the Final Part of the Days"

predecessors, Zedekiah "continued to do what was bad in the eyes of Jehovah." (Jer. 52:1, 2) He was a subject of the Babylonians, and Nebuchadnezzar made him take an oath in Jehovah's name that obliged him to submit to the king of Babylon. Despite that, Zedekiah eventually rebelled. Meanwhile, Jeremiah's enemies exerted great pressure on him to support the rebellion.—2 Chron. 36:13; Ezek. 17:12, 13.

²¹ Evidently early in the reign of Zedekiah, messengers arrived in Jerusalem from the kings of Edom, Moab, Ammon, Tyre, and Sidon. Perhaps their aim was to get Zedekiah to join a coalition against Nebuchadnezzar. Jeremiah, however, urged Zedekiah to submit to Babylon. In line with that, Jeremiah presented the messengers with yoke bars to picture that their nations too should serve the Babylonians. (Jer. 27:1-3, 14)\* That stance was not popular, and Jeremiah's role as a spokesman with an unpopular message was made no easier by Hananiah. He was a false prophet who publicly asserted in God's name that the Babylonian yoke would be broken. Jehovah's word through Jeremiah, however, was that within a year, the impostor Hananiah would die. That is what occurred.—Jer. 28:1-3, 16, 17.

²² Judah was now split into opposing factions—those who favored submission to Babylon and those who urged rebellion. In 609 B.C.E., Zedekiah did rebel by seeking military assistance from Egypt. Jeremiah then had to contend with the nationalistic hysteria of those

---

\* The reference to Jehoiakim at Jeremiah 27:1 may be a transcriber's error because verses 3 and 12 refer to Zedekiah.

---

21-23. (a) What opposing factions could be found in Judah during Zedekiah's reign? (b) How was Jeremiah treated because of his stance, and why should that interest you?

supporting the rebellion. (Jer. 52:3; Ezek. 17:15) Nebuchadnezzar and his armies returned to Judah to quell the revolt, conquering all the cities of Judah and again besieging Jerusalem. Jeremiah's message to Zedekiah and his subjects at this critical time was that Jerusalem would fall to the Babylonians. Death awaited those who remained in the city. Those who went out to the Chaldeans would survive.—*Read Jeremiah 21:8-10; 52:4.*

²³ The princes of Judah claimed that Jeremiah was throwing in his lot with the Babylonians. When he stated the truth, the Judean princes struck him and put him in the house of detention. (Jer. 37:13-15) Jeremiah would still not soften Jehovah's message. Therefore, the princes persuaded Zedekiah to put Jeremiah to death. They put the prophet into an empty water cistern where he could have perished in the deep mire. But Ebed-melech, an Ethiopian serving in the king's house, rescued Jeremiah. (Jer. 38:4-13) How often Jehovah's people in modern times have faced perils because of their conscientious refusal to get involved in political controversies! Clearly, Jeremiah's experience can fortify you to face trials and overcome them.

²⁴ In 607 B.C.E., the Babylonians finally broke through Jerusalem's walls, and the city fell. Nebuchadnezzar's forces burned Jehovah's temple, demolished the city walls, and slaughtered the nobles of Judah. Zedekiah attempted to flee, only to be captured and brought before his conqueror. Zedekiah's sons were slaughtered before his eyes, and then Nebuchadnezzar had him blinded, bound, and led away to Babylon. (Jer. 39:1-7) Yes, Jeremiah's words regarding Judah and Jerusalem

---

24. Describe the events of 607 B.C.E.

## ZEDEKIAH—THE LAST EARTHLY KING OF JUDAH

Zedekiah was a spineless, vacillating ruler dominated by his princes and his own fears. During the final Babylonian siege of Jerusalem, Zedekiah sought God's guidance from Jeremiah. Yet, the king failed to act in harmony with it when told to surrender. Because he did not like Jeremiah's message, Zedekiah imprisoned him. (Jer. 21:1-9; 32:1-5) Nonetheless, the king continued to consult Jeremiah but in secret so as not to upset Judah's princes. When they sought Jeremiah's death, Zedekiah weakly acquiesced, saying: "He is in your hands. For there is nothing at all in which the king himself can prevail against you." After Jeremiah was released from the threat of death, the king again consulted him and admitted that he feared that if he obeyed God, the people would mistreat him.—Jer. 37:15-17; 38:4, 5, 14-19, 24-26.

Still, Zedekiah "did not humble himself on account of Jeremiah . . . , and he kept stiffening his neck and hardening his heart so as not to return to Jehovah." —2 Chron. 36:12, 13; Ezek. 21:25.

had come true. Rather than rejoice, God's prophet mourned the calamity of his people. We can read his sentiments in the Bible book of Lamentations. We should be deeply touched as we read that book.

## ACTIVITY AMONG A REMNANT OF JUDAH

<sup>25</sup> What was happening to Jeremiah as these dramatic events unfolded? The princes of Jerusalem had imprisoned him, but the conquering Babylonians treated him kindly, freeing him. Later, Jeremiah got mixed in with some Jews being taken off into captivity, but he was released. There was yet more for him to do in God's service; he still had work to do among the survivors. Nebuchadnezzar appointed Gedaliah as governor over the conquered land, promising the remaining Judeans peace as long as they served him, the king of Babylon. Some malcontent Jews, however, assassinated Gedaliah. (Jer. 39:13, 14; 40:1-7; 41:2) Jeremiah urged the remnant of Judeans to keep dwelling in the land and not to fear the king of Babylon. Their leaders, however, called Jeremiah a liar and fled to Egypt, forcibly taking along Jeremiah and Baruch. Yet, Jeremiah prophesied that Nebuchadnezzar would invade and subdue even that country and bring calamity on the Judean refugees.—Jer. 42:9-11; 43:1-11; 44:11-13.

<sup>26</sup> Once again, the response of Jeremiah's fellow countrymen was not to listen to God's true prophet. Why? "From the time that we ceased to make sacrificial smoke to the 'queen of the heavens' and pour out drink offerings to her," they reasoned, "we have lacked everything, and by the sword and by the famine we have come to

---

25, 26. (a) What events followed the fall of Jerusalem? (b) How did Jeremiah's contemporaries react to his message after Jerusalem fell?

*Serving in "the Final Part of the Days"* 31

our finish." (Jer. 44:16, 18) What a sad reflection of the spiritual state of Jeremiah's contemporaries! On the other hand, how encouraging it should be to us to know that an imperfect human can remain faithful to Jehovah despite being surrounded by the faithless!

²⁷ The last event that Jeremiah recorded—the release from prison of Jehoiachin at the hands of Nebuchadnezzar's successor, Evil-merodach—is dated 580 B.C.E. (Jer. 52:31-34) By this time, Jeremiah must have been about 90 years old. We have no reliable information concerning the end of his life. It is likely that he lived out his final years in Egypt and died faithful there after some 67 years in special service to Jehovah. He served during years when true worship was promoted as well as during many years when apostate worship was all around him. He did find listening ears among some God-fearing people. The majority, though, rejected his messages, even displaying outright hostility. Did that make Jeremiah a failure? Far from it! Right from the beginning, Jehovah had told him: "They will be certain to fight against you, but they will not prevail against you, for 'I am with you.'" (Jer. 1:19) Our commission as Jehovah's Witnesses today is like that of Jeremiah. So we can expect the reception to be similar. (*Read Matthew 10:16-22.*) Therefore, what lessons can we learn from Jeremiah, and how should we approach our ministry? Let us consider these questions.

---

27. What do we know about the final years of Jeremiah's prophetic career?

*What happened to Zedekiah and his subjects who rejected Jeremiah's message? What is your view of Jeremiah?*

## Chapter Three

# "You Must Say to Them This Word"

JESUS CHRIST is the chief model whom we follow in preaching the good news. It is noteworthy, though, that people in the first century who observed Jesus sometimes thought of the prophet Jeremiah. (Matt. 16:13, 14) As was true of Jesus, Jeremiah received a divine command to preach. For example, on one occasion God told him: "You must say to them this word, 'This is what Jehovah . . . has said.'" (Jer. 13:12, 13; John 12:49) And in his ministry Jeremiah displayed qualities similar to those of Jesus.

[2] However, some Witnesses might say: 'Our preaching work is different from that of Jeremiah. He was God's spokesman to a nation that was dedicated to Him, while most of those to whom we preach do not know Jehovah.' That is true. But by Jeremiah's time, most Jews had become "unwise" and had left the true God. (*Read Jeremiah 5:20-22.*) They needed to change to worship Jehovah acceptably. Similarly, people today—whether claiming to be Christian or not—need to learn to fear Jehovah and pursue true worship. Let us see how we can serve the true God and help people by imitating Jeremiah.

---

1. (a) How were Jesus and Jeremiah similar? (b) Why should we imitate Jeremiah in our ministry?
2. How are the needs of people today similar to those of the Jews in Jeremiah's time?

## 'JEHOVAH TOUCHED MY MOUTH'

³ Recall that at the start of his prophetic ministry, Jeremiah heard these words: "To all those to whom I shall send you, you should go; and everything that I shall command you, you should speak. Do not be afraid because of their faces, for 'I am with you to deliver you,' is the utterance of Jehovah." (Jer. 1:7, 8) And then God made an unexpected gesture. Jeremiah tells us: "Jehovah thrust his hand out and caused it to touch my mouth. Then Jehovah said to me: 'Here I have put my words in your mouth. See, I have commissioned you this day.'" (Jer. 1:9, 10) From then on, Jeremiah knew that he spoke for Almighty God.* With His full support, Jeremiah's zeal for sacred service grew.—Isa. 6:5-8.

---

* As in this case, Jehovah often had angelic messengers present themselves as though He were speaking.—Judg. 13:15, 22; Gal. 3:19.

---

3. What meaningful gesture did God make toward Jeremiah at the beginning of his work, and how did the prophet feel about it?

[4] Jehovah does not physically touch any of his servants today. Yet, through his spirit, he does give them a strong desire to preach the good news. Many of them glow with zeal. Take the case of Maruja in Spain. For over 40 years, her arms and legs have been paralyzed. Preaching from door to door is difficult for her, so she finds other ways to be active in the ministry. One way is by writing letters. Maruja dictates the words to her daughter, who writes them down. During a month-long campaign, Maruja and her "secretary" sent out over 150 letters, enclosing a copy of a tract in each envelope. Through their efforts, the good news reached most of the homes in a nearby village. Maruja commented to her daughter, "If one of our letters gets into the hands of a person with an upright heart, Jehovah will bless us with a Bible study." A local elder writes, "I thank Jehovah for sisters like Maruja, who teach others to value what is really important."

---

4. What examples of outstanding zeal in preaching can you relate?

⁵ In Jeremiah's time, most of Jerusalem's inhabitants took "no delight" in God's truth. Did the prophet stop preaching because so many were apathetic about the message? On the contrary! Jeremiah said: "With the rage of Jehovah I have become full. I have become weary with holding in." (Jer. 6:10, 11) How can you maintain zeal like that? One way is to meditate on the incomparable privilege you have of representing the true God. You know that prominent ones in this world have reproached the name of the true God. Think, too, of how religious leaders have deceived the people of your territory, even as the priests did in Jeremiah's day. (*Read Jeremiah 2:8, 26, 27.*) In contrast, the good news of God's Kingdom that you declare is really an expression of God's favor toward humanity. (Lam. 3:31, 32) Yes, reflecting on such truth can help you maintain your zeal for declaring the good news and helping sheeplike ones.

⁶ You will likely agree that maintaining zeal in the Christian ministry is not always easy. As he served Jehovah, Jeremiah too met with serious challenges, including false prophets. You can read of one instance in Jeremiah chapter 28. Most of the people paid no heed to his message, and sometimes he felt rather isolated. (Jer. 6:16, 17; 15:17) Moreover, on occasion he had to cope with enemies who threatened his life.—Jer. 26:11.

---

5. (a) How did Jeremiah maintain his zeal in the face of apathy? (b) How can you maintain your zeal for preaching the good news?
6. Jeremiah faced what daunting challenges?

***Why can you trust Jehovah to help you overcome challenges as you preach the good news?***

## "YOU HAVE FOOLED ME, O JEHOVAH"

⁷ During one period when Jeremiah faced mockery and insults day after day, he expressed his feelings to God. In what sense, do you think, can you say that Jehovah "fooled" his faithful prophet, as mentioned at Jeremiah 20:7, 8?—*Read.*

⁸ Jehovah had definitely not tricked or deceived Jeremiah by using some crafty, underhanded scheme against him. Rather, God "fooled" his prophet in a positive, beneficial sense. Jeremiah felt that the opposition was too great, that by himself he could no longer fulfill his God-given assignment. But fulfill it he did, with the Almighty's support and help. Hence, you might say that Jehovah overpowered him, proving far stronger than Jeremiah and his human inclinations. When this man of God thought that he had reached his limit and could not keep going, Jehovah exercised a persuasive force so that Jeremiah was fooled, as it were. God proved stronger than the prophet's weaknesses. Even in the face of apathy, rejection, and violence, Jeremiah was able to continue to preach.

⁹ Jehovah proved to be like "a terrible mighty one" alongside Jeremiah, supporting him. (Jer. 20:11) And God can strengthen you too so that you keep your zeal for true worship and carry on despite major problems. You might think of it as it is expressed in another translation—Jehovah will be "a mighty soldier" standing at your side.—*Contemporary English Version.*

¹⁰ The apostle Paul underscored that point when encouraging Christians who faced opposition. He wrote:

---

7, 8. In what beneficial way did God 'fool' Jeremiah?
9. Why can you take courage from the words of Jeremiah 20:11?
10. What are you determined to do when facing opposition?

"Behave in a manner worthy of the good news about the Christ, in order that . . . I may hear . . . that you are standing firm in one spirit, with one soul striving side by side for the faith of the good news, and in no respect being frightened by your opponents." (Phil. 1:27, 28) As did Jeremiah and Christians in the first century, you can and should lean on Almighty God as you carry out your ministry. If some people deride or attack you, remember that Jehovah is at your side and can fill you with power. He did so for Jeremiah and has done so for many of your brothers; hence, he can do so for you. Supplicate him for help, and trust that he will respond to your prayer. You too may find that you are "fooled" as God gives you strength to face obstacles successfully, with boldness instead of fear. Yes, you may do far more than you ever thought possible.—*Read Acts 4:29-31.*

[11] What we read of Jeremiah's service can help us in various ways to be more effective ministers of the good news. After he had served as Jehovah's prophet for over 20 years, he was able to say: "I kept speaking to you people, rising up early and speaking, but you did not listen." (Jer. 25:3) Yes, he got an early start rather than a late one. Can we learn something practical from his example? In many congregations, there are publishers who rise early to speak with people at bus stops and train stations. In rural areas, many Witnesses use the early hours of the day to visit farmers and others who are active at that time. Can you think of other ways that you personally can apply this lesson from Jeremiah's faithful ministry? What about getting up sufficiently early to be present right at the start of a scheduled meeting for field service?

---

11, 12. (a) What adjustments might you make in order to speak with more people in your ministry? (b) What local possibilities does the photograph on page 39 suggest?

¹² Moreover, preaching from door to door in the afternoon and evening often produces excellent results in many localities. Some publishers even preach at night, visiting workers at gas stations, restaurants, and other businesses that are open 24 hours a day. Can you adjust your schedule so that you can preach when you are most likely to find people at home or elsewhere?

*Why do you feel confident that Jehovah is backing you as you proclaim his message?*

---

¹³ On occasion, Jehovah commanded Jeremiah to announce prophetic messages while standing in the gates of the temple or of Jerusalem. (Jer. 7:2; 17:19, 20) By making such declarations at the gates, Jeremiah reached large numbers of people with Jehovah's word. And since many, including prominent men of the city, merchants, and businessmen, used the same gate habitually, he may have spoken to some people repeatedly in an effort to help them understand what they had previously heard. What can we learn from this about making return visits on those who have shown interest?

¹⁴ Jeremiah knew that lives depended on his work as God's prophet. Once, when he could not carry out divine instructions to speak with the people, he sent his friend Baruch in his place. (*Read Jeremiah 36:5-8.*) How can we imitate Jeremiah in this? When we tell a householder that we will return, do we keep our word? If we cannot keep an appointment for a return visit or a home Bible study, do we arrange for a substitute? Jesus said:

---

13, 14. (a) How does Jeremiah's example relate to making return visits? (b) What illustrates your need to be dependable about making return visits?

*"You Must Say to Them This Word"*

*Have you adjusted your schedule and preaching methods so that you can witness to more people?*

"Let your word *Yes* mean Yes." (Matt. 5:37) Keeping our word is essential, for we represent the God of truth and order.—1 Cor. 14:33, 40.

¹⁵ Jeremiah encouraged the Jews in Babylon by writing them a letter about Jehovah's "good word" of restoration. (Jer. 29:1-4, 10) Today, the "good word" of what Jehovah will soon do can also be effectively spread by letter and telephone. Could you use those methods to help your relatives or others who are in faraway places or who are difficult to contact?

¹⁶ By following Jeremiah's example of fully accomplishing his ministry, Kingdom publishers today often

---

15, 16. (a) How have many followed Jeremiah's example in expanding their ministry? (b) What lesson do you see in the experience from Chile, depicted on page 40?

*Do you make the necessary effort to cultivate all the interest you have found?*

obtain positive results. A Witness in Chile approached a woman exiting a subway station. She was thrilled to hear the Bible's message and agreed to a Bible discussion at her home. The Witness, however, did not write down the woman's address. Afterward, realizing the importance of cultivating the woman's interest in the truth, our sister prayed to Jehovah for help. The next day, she returned to the subway station at the same hour. She met the woman again. This time, she took care to write down her address and later visited the woman at her home to help her understand the Scriptures. God's judgments are soon to overtake Satan's world. But there is hope for those who repent and put faith in the good news. (*Read Lamentations 3:31-33.*) Hence, let us reflect that fact by conscientiously working our territory.

## "PERHAPS THEY WILL LISTEN AND RETURN, EACH ONE"

17 Jehovah did not want people to lose their lives. Some ten years before Jerusalem's destruction, he used Jeremiah to outline a hope for those exiled in Babylon. We read: "I will set my eye upon them in a good way, and I shall certainly cause them to return to this land. And I will build them up, and I shall not tear down; and I will plant them, and I shall not uproot." Jeremiah could say to such ones: "There exists a hope for your future." (Jer. 24:6; 26:3; 31:17) Jeremiah made God's view of people his own. He carried out his ministry with genuine concern, conveying Jehovah's urgings: "Turn back, please, each one from his bad way, and make your dealings good." (Jer. 35:15) Can you think of additional ways to show deep personal interest in people in your territory?

18 Jeremiah's deep love for the people never cooled off. At Jerusalem's destruction, he continued to feel compassion for them. (*Read Lamentations 2:11.*) The Jews had themselves to blame for their disaster. Jeremiah, however, did not say, 'I told you so.' Rather, he felt great sadness for what had overtaken them. Similarly, our ministry must not become perfunctory, done only out of obligation. Our efforts at giving a witness should prove how much we love our wonderful God as well as people, who are created in his image.

19 No privilege or position in this world can surpass that of witnessing on behalf of the true God. Jeremiah felt that way, writing: "Your words were found, and

---

17. In your territory, how can you imitate Jeremiah's approach?
18, 19. (a) What view must we reject as we preach the good news? (b) What attitude of Jeremiah should we make our own?

*Do you show people that
you are interested in their welfare?*

I proceeded to eat them; and your word becomes to me the exultation and the rejoicing of my heart; for your name has been called upon me, O Jehovah." (Jer. 15:16) As we preach the good news, many more may come to know and love the One to whom they owe their lives. By serving with zeal and love, as exemplified by Jeremiah, we will contribute to that end.

*Given Jeremiah's example, what additional ways to spread Jehovah's "good word" might you try in the future?*

## Chapter Four

# GUARD AGAINST A TREACHEROUS HEART

SUPPOSE that early one morning while still in bed, you felt an acute pain in the middle of your chest and had shortness of breath. You might wonder, 'Could it be a heart attack?' Just denying the problem would not help. Immediate action would be in order. So you might call for an ambulance in order to get expert medical care. A physician might carefully examine you, perhaps employing an electrocardiogram. Prompt diagnosis and treatment could mean the difference between life and death.

[2] How about our figurative heart? It may not be easy to know its real condition. Why? We read in the Bible: "The heart is more treacherous than anything else and is desperate. Who can know it?" (Jer. 17:9) So our heart can deceive us, leading us to believe that no real spiritual problem exists, while others may see warning signs and be concerned. Why might we be deceived? Well, our sinful inclinations may work against us, as Satan and this system of things mask our real situation. As for examining our heart, we can learn from Jeremiah and the people of Judah in his day.

[3] The majority of the Judeans had shown that their hearts were spiritually defective. They left the only

---

1, 2. Why is it difficult to know the real condition of our figurative heart?
3. What have become gods for many people?

true God for Canaanite gods, feeling no qualms of conscience. Jehovah challenged those worshippers: "Where are your gods that you have made for yourself? Let them rise up if they can save you in the time of your calamity. For as the number of your cities your gods have become." (Jer. 2:28) In our case, we certainly do not think of ourselves as worshippers of idol gods. However, under the heading "god," one dictionary says: "A person or thing of supreme value." Many people in the world place first in life their career, health, family, and even pets. Others consider sports, celebrities, technology, travel, or their traditions to be of supreme value. Many pursue such things at the cost of their relationship with the Creator. Could true Christians be affected, even as were people of Judah in Jeremiah's day?

## TREACHEROUS HEARTS CAN DECEIVE

⁴ You will likely find interesting the context of Jeremiah's statement describing the heart as desperate. He realized that people were saying: "Where is the word of Jehovah? Let it come in, please." (Jer. 17:15) But were they sincere? Well, that chapter of Jeremiah opens this way: "The sin of Judah is written down with an iron stylus. With a diamond point it is engraved on the tablet of their heart." A key problem was that those Judeans were 'putting their trust in earthling man, making flesh their arm, and turning their heart away from Jehovah.' That was in contrast to the minority, who trusted in God, looking to him for guidance and blessings.—Jer. 17:1, 5, 7.

⁵ The hearts of the majority were revealed in their reac-

---

4. How sincere were the people who said: "Where is the word of Jehovah? Let it come in"?
5. In what ways did Jeremiah's countrymen respond to Jehovah's direction?

*Guard Against a Treacherous Heart*                                            45

tion to what God said. (*Read Jeremiah 17:21, 22.*) For example, the Sabbath was to be a rest from regular labor and an opportunity to share in spiritual activities. Jeremiah's countrymen were not to conduct business or run errands on the Sabbath. But their response revealed the condition of their heart. "They did not listen or incline their ear, and they proceeded to harden their neck in order not to hear and in order to receive no discipline." Although they knew God's law, they had their own view —they had things to do on the Sabbath.—Jer. 17:23; Isa. 58:13.

⁶ Today, we are not under Sabbath law. Yet, there is a warning lesson in the way those people reacted, showing their heart condition. (Col. 2:16) In order to do God's will, we have put aside our selfish or mundane pursuits. We realize how foolish it would be to choose for ourselves a convenient way to please God. And we have likely come to know many who have concentrated on doing God's will and have indeed found that to be refreshing, restful. Hence, how might we be misled?

⁷ A Christian might mistakenly think that his heart could never deceive him, as happened to many in Jeremiah's day. For example, a man might reason, 'I have to hold down a job to support my family,' which is understandable. What if that led him to think, 'I need more education to secure or hold a decent job'? That too might seem logical, leading him to conclude, 'Times have changed, and to survive today you need to get a college or university education to hold on to your job.' How easily one might start to minimize the wise,

---

6, 7. (a) How might a Christian unwisely reason, despite counsel from the faithful slave class today? (b) How might our meeting attendance be affected?

balanced advice from the faithful and discreet slave class about additional education and start to miss meetings! In this area, some have gradually been molded by the world's reasonings and views. (Eph. 2:2, 3) The Bible aptly warns us: "Don't let the world around you squeeze you into its own mould."—Rom. 12:2, *Phillips.*\*

⁸ Granted, some Christians in the first century had riches and perhaps a bit of prominence in the world. That is true of some Christians in our time too. How

---

\* The *NET Bible* (2005) reads: "Do not be conformed to this present world." A footnote adds: "It is very telling that being 'conformed' to the present world is viewed as a passive notion, for it may suggest that it happens, in part, subconsciously. At the same time, . . . there may be some consciousness of the conformity taking place. Most likely, it is a combination of both."

---

8. (a) About what might a Christian feel some pride? (b) Why is more needed than knowing facts about God and his dealings?

*Has your heart deceived you into missing meetings?*

should they feel about their accomplishments, and how should we view such ones? Jehovah provided the answer through Jeremiah. (*Read Jeremiah 9:23, 24.*) Rather than bragging about human accomplishments, a person is wise to acknowledge that knowing the Universal Sovereign is of chief value. (1 Cor. 1:31) What, though, does it mean to have insight and knowledge of Jehovah? Well, the people of Jeremiah's day knew God's name. They were also aware of what he did in saving their ancestors at the Red Sea, during the entry into the Promised Land, in the times of the Judges, and during the reigns of faithful kings. Nevertheless, they did not really know Jehovah or exercise genuine faith in him. Yet, they said: "I have remained innocent. Surely [God's] anger has turned back from me."—Jer. 2:35.

*Why is it important to recognize that our heart is treacherous? How can we examine our heart and learn how the Great Examiner of hearts might view us?*

## THE WAY JEHOVAH MOLDS US

9 The Jews to whom Jeremiah delivered God's message needed a change of heart. That was possible because God said of those who would return from exile: "I will give them a heart to know me, that I am Jehovah; and they must become my people, and I myself shall become their God, for they will return to me." (Jer. 24:7) A similar change is possible today too. Moreover, most of us can improve the condition of our spiritual heart. Three things are vital: serious personal study of God's Word, insight into how God works in our own life, and

---

9. Why can we be sure that a change of heart is possible, and how can it come about?

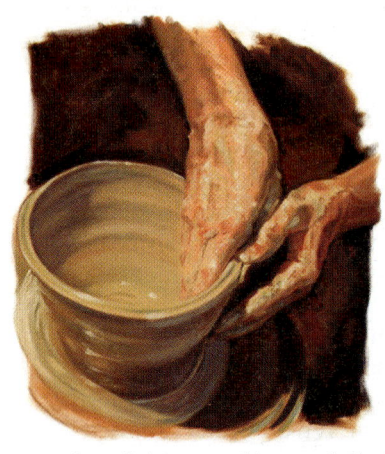

*Are you letting Jehovah mold you?*

application of what we have learned about him. Unlike those in Jeremiah's day, we should want to have our heart inspected by the Great Examiner of hearts. And we can examine our own heart in the light of the Bible as well as by noting how Jehovah has acted in our behalf. (Ps. 17:3) How wise it is to do so!

¹⁰ Satan wants to shape people by squeezing them all into a certain mold, but molding by God takes individuals into account. We see this illustrated in Jeremiah's experience. One day, God told him to go to the house of a potter. The potter was working at his wheel, but when the vessel he was forming was spoiled, he simply molded the still-moist clay into a different vessel. (*Read Jeremiah 18:1-4.*) Why was Jeremiah directed to watch this, and what can we learn from his experience?

¹¹ Jehovah wanted to show Jeremiah and Israel that He has authority to shape peoples and nations into what He wants. How does God handle the clay? Unlike human potters, Jehovah does not make mistakes; nor does he destroy the works of his hand on a whim. How people respond to being molded by Jehovah determines what he does with them.—*Read Jeremiah 18:6-10.*

---

10, 11. (a) Why did Jeremiah go to see a potter? (b) What determines how Jehovah molds people?

## Guard Against a Treacherous Heart

¹² How, then, does Jehovah mold individuals? Foremost today, he uses the Bible. As a person reads and responds to God's Word, he reveals what kind of person he is, and God can mold him. Let us now consider the example of King Jehoiakim to see how people in Jeremiah's day might have been molded in matters of daily life. The Law decreed that one "must not defraud a hired laborer," yet the king did just that, exploiting fellow Israelites by using them as a source of cheap labor to build "a roomy house." (Deut. 24:14; Jer. 22:13, 14, 17) God tried to mold Jehoiakim by means of His word delivered by the prophets. Yet, the king followed the inclination of his treacherous heart. He said, "I shall not obey" and held to the way he had taken from his youth on. Thus, God said: "With the burial of a he-ass [Jehoiakim] will be buried, with a dragging about and a throwing away." (Jer. 22:19, 21) How foolish it would be for us to respond: 'That is just how I am'! Today, God is not sending prophets like Jeremiah, but He does offer guidance. The faithful and discreet slave class helps us to see and apply Bible principles. These may touch aspects of daily life, such as our dress and grooming or the music and dancing linked to a wedding or to another social event. Will we allow ourselves to be molded by God's Word?

¹³ Consider another example. The Babylonians put Zedekiah on the throne of Judah as a vassal king. Then, contrary to God's advice through Jeremiah, Zedekiah rebelled. (Jer. 27:8, 12) So the Babylonians besieged Jerusalem. The king and his princes felt that they should

---

12. (a) How did Jehoiakim respond to Jehovah's efforts to mold him? (b) What lesson do you see in the account about Jehoiakim?
13, 14. (a) Why did slave owners in Jerusalem agree to free their Hebrew slaves? (b) What revealed the real heart condition of the slave owners?

do something to comply with the Law to gain God's favor. Aware that Hebrew slaves were to be released in the seventh year of their bondage, Zedekiah concluded a covenant to liberate such slaves. (Ex. 21:2; Jer. 34:14) Yes, with Jerusalem surrounded by enemies, it suddenly seemed advisable for the people to free their slaves! —*Read Jeremiah 34:8-10.*

[14] Later, an Egyptian military force came to Jerusalem's aid, causing the Babylonians to lift the siege. (Jer. 37:5) What would those who had freed their slaves do? They forced back into servitude those whom they had emancipated. (Jer. 34:11) The point is that when they were in danger, the Jews seemed to observe divine statutes, as if that could offset their former conduct. But when the danger subsided, they went back to their old ways. Despite their pretense of accepting the spirit of the Law, their later actions revealed that at heart they did not want to comply with direction found in God's Word and be molded by it.

*What practical lesson can you take away from what Jeremiah wrote about a potter? How does Jehovah mold us today?*

## ACCEPT MOLDING BY JEHOVAH

[15] With the help of Jehovah's worldwide congregation, we may become aware of Bible principles that deal with a specific course. For instance, we might know how we ought to respond if a brother seems to rub us the wrong way. (Eph. 4:32) We might admit that the Bible's counsel is right and wise. Yet, what kind of clay will we prove to

---

15. To what extent would you like to be molded by Jehovah? Illustrate.

be? Will we really respond to being molded by Jehovah? If our heart is malleable, we will change for the better; the Great Potter will mold us into a vessel more suitable for his use. (*Read Romans 9:20, 21; 2 Timothy 2:20, 21.*) Rather than show a heart attitude like that of Jehoiakim or the slave owners in Zedekiah's day, we should accept being molded by Jehovah for an honorable purpose.

¹⁶ Even Jeremiah was molded by God. What was the prophet's attitude? You can tell from his admission: "It does not belong to man who is walking even to direct his step." He then pleaded: "Correct me, O Jehovah." (Jer. 10: 23, 24) Young ones, will you imitate Jeremiah? You likely have many decisions ahead of you. Some youths want to 'direct their own step.' Will you look to God for guidance when making decisions? Will you, like Jeremiah, humbly admit that humans have proved incapable of directing their own steps? Remember: If you seek God's direction, he will mold you.

¹⁷ Jeremiah's assignment involved obedience to God's direction. If you had been Jeremiah, would you have accepted any such instructions given? At one point, Jehovah told Jeremiah to get a linen belt and wear it. Next, God commanded him to travel to the Euphrates. Consult a map, and you will see that this meant a trip of some 300 miles. Once there, Jeremiah was to hide the belt in the cleft of a crag and then travel all the way back to Jerusalem. And God later had him return to get the belt. (*Read Jeremiah 13:1-9.*) In all, Jeremiah would have traveled about 1,200 miles. Bible critics just cannot believe

---

16. Jeremiah was aware of what important truth?
17-19. (a) Why did Jeremiah make a long trip to the Euphrates? (b) How could Jeremiah's obedience have been under test? (c) What was accomplished by Jeremiah's actions involving the belt?

that he would travel so far, walking for months.* (Ezra 7:9) Still, that is what God said and what Jeremiah did.

[18] Picture the prophet trekking through the Judean mountains and then, depending on his route, into a desert toward the Euphrates. All of that just to hide a linen belt! His long absence must have aroused the curiosity of his neighbors. When he returned, he did not have the linen belt with him. Then God told him to make the long trip again, to retrieve the belt, now rotten and "not fit for anything." Imagine how easy it would have been to think: 'Now that is just too much. I see no point to it.' Yet, having been molded by God, he did not react that way. Rather than complain, he did as he was instructed!

[19] It was only after the second journey that God explained matters. Jeremiah's actions set the stage for him to deliver a potent message: "This bad people who are refusing to obey my words, who are walking in the stubbornness of their heart and who keep walking after other gods in order to serve them and to bow down to them, will also become just like this belt that is fit for nothing." (Jer. 13:10) What an impressive way for Jehovah to teach his people! Jeremiah's heartfelt obedience to Jehovah in what may have seemed trivial played a role in His efforts to reach the hearts of the people.—Jer. 13:11.

[20] Christians today are not being asked to walk hundreds of miles as part of a divine lesson. Might it be, though, that the Christian course you pursue could cause

---

* Some consider Jeremiah's destination to be nearby instead of at the Euphrates. Why? "The sole object of this criticism," states one scholar, "is to save the prophet the labour of two supposed journeys from Jerusalem to the Euphrates."

---

20. Why might your obedience puzzle some, but of what can you be sure?

*Why should we obey Jehovah's instructions even if we do not fully understand them?*

neighbors or associates to be puzzled or even to criticize you? It may involve your dress and grooming, your choice as to education, what you prefer as a career, or even your view of alcoholic beverages. Will you be as determined to comply with God's guidance as Jeremiah was? Your choices because of allowing your heart to be molded by God may lead to your giving a fine witness. In any case, being obedient to Jehovah's direction found in his Word and accepting the guidance given through the faithful slave class is for your lasting good. Rather than being led by a treacherous heart, you can be like Jeremiah. Be resolved, then, to accept being molded by God; let him form you into an honorable vessel for his lasting use.

*Why is it vital to fight pressures from Satan, from our imperfect heart, and from the world?*

## CHAPTER FIVE

# WHAT FRIENDS WILL YOU CHOOSE?

WHAT would you do if some colleagues, neighbors, or schoolmates invited you to attend a Christmas party? Suppose your employer asked you to lie or to do something illegal? Or what if governmental authorities called on you to engage in nonneutral activities? Your conscience would likely tell you not to do any of these things, even if as a result of your refusal, you might be ridiculed or treated worse.

[2] As we will see, Jeremiah often found himself facing similar challenges. You can certainly benefit from considering some of the individuals and groups with whom Jeremiah came in contact during his years of service. Some of them tried to discourage him from carrying out his commission. Jeremiah had to have some close contact with them, but they were definitely not his chosen friends. You can, however, profitably note the friends whom Jeremiah did choose, those who supported him and encouraged his resolve to be faithful. Yes, we can learn from Jeremiah's decisions involving companions.

---

1, 2. (a) What challenges do Christians face regarding companions? (b) Why should we be interested in Jeremiah's choice of friends?

## WHAT FRIENDSHIPS DO YOU CULTIVATE?

³ King Zedekiah consulted Jeremiah on a number of occasions prior to the destruction of Jerusalem. Why? The king hoped to receive reassuring responses to inquiries about the future of his realm. He wanted Jeremiah

---

3. What did Zedekiah want from Jeremiah, and how did Jeremiah respond?

---

When you read about Jeremiah and Ebed-melech, are you confident that they were real people? Recently, the account in Jeremiah chapter 38 that mentions them gained added support from two discoveries made in the ancient City of David.

Archaeologist Eilat Mazar reports unearthing a small clay seal impression, or bulla. (below left) It was found in 2005 during a supervised excavation of a layer dating back to when Jerusalem was destroyed in 607 B.C.E. The seal bears the ancient Hebrew name "Yehuchal ben Shelemyahu," which is "Jucal the son of Shelemiah" in English.

Later, in a similar layer and just a few yards away, another bulla was uncovered. (below right) It bears the name "Gedalyahu ben Pashhur," or "Gedaliah the son of Pashhur."

Now read at Jeremiah 38:1 the names of two princes who urged King Zedekiah to have Jeremiah put to death, a plan that Ebed-melech thwarted. Yes, those named in Jeremiah chapter 38 were real people.

to announce that divine intervention would save Judah from her enemies. Through emissaries, Zedekiah petitioned Jeremiah: "Please inquire in our behalf of Jehovah, because Nebuchadrezzar the king of Babylon is making war against us. Perhaps Jehovah will do with us according to all his wonderful works, so that [Nebuchadrezzar] will withdraw from us." (Jer. 21:2) The king did not want to follow God's direction to surrender to Babylon. One scholar likened Zedekiah to "a patient returning again and again to a doctor in search of reassurance, yet unwilling to take the medicine prescribed." What about Jeremiah? He could have become popular by telling Zedekiah what he wanted to hear. Why, then, did Jeremiah not just change his message and make his life easier? He refused to do so because Jehovah had told him to proclaim that Jerusalem would fall.—*Read Jeremiah 32:1-5.*

⁴ In some ways your situation is like Jeremiah's. No doubt you have contact with neighbors, workmates, or schoolmates who in a sense are associates or companions. But will you take matters further, cultivating friendships with them even though they have shown that they are not interested in hearing or following God's direction? Jeremiah could not shun Zedekiah altogether; he was still the king, even when refusing to follow God's counsel. Jeremiah was not obliged, though, to conform to the king's misguided thinking or to curry his favor. Granted, if Jeremiah had complied with the king's wishes, Zedekiah could have showered him with gifts and other benefits. Jeremiah nevertheless refused to give in to any pressure or temptation to be close to

---

4. What decisions do we face about cultivating friendships, such as at our place of work?

Zedekiah. Why? Because Jeremiah was not about to alter the stance that Jehovah had told him to adopt. Jeremiah's example should move us to examine whether those whom we chose as friends are encouraging us to be loyal to God. You cannot avoid all contact with people who are not serving God—those at work, at school, or in your neighborhood. (1 Cor. 5:9, 10) You realize, however, that if you choose such ones as friends, you might well compromise your friendship with God.

## KEEPING COMPANY WITH SKEPTICS?

5 Zedekiah was not the only one who tried to exercise a negative influence on Jeremiah. A priest named Pashhur "struck" Jeremiah, perhaps having him beaten with 39 strokes. (Jer. 20:2; Deut. 25:3) Some Judean princes did a similar thing and then imprisoned Jeremiah in

---

5, 6. What did some do in an attempt to silence Jeremiah?

"the house of fetters." The prophet was put in a dungeon under conditions so bad that after many days he feared he would die there. (*Read Jeremiah 37:3, 15, 16.*) Then, after Jeremiah had been set free for a while, other princes urged Zedekiah to execute him. In their view, he was demoralizing Judah's troops. That led to the prophet's being flung into a miry cistern to die. (Jer. 38:1-4) You have read that Jeremiah was saved from that horrible death. Yet, these events illustrate how those who should have known better became skeptical of what God's prophet had to say; they turned on him.

⁶ Jeremiah's enemies were not limited to the civil authorities. On another occasion, some men from Jeremiah's home city of Anathoth—his neighbors, you might say—threatened to kill him if he did not stop prophesying. (Jer. 11:21) They did not like what they heard from him and they threatened him. Jeremiah, though, chose as his friend Jehovah rather than neighbors. Other contemporaries went beyond words. When

Jeremiah graphically used a yoke to urge the Jews to bring their necks under the yoke of the king of Babylon and thus keep living, Hananiah removed the wooden yoke from Jeremiah's neck and broke it. According to that false prophet, Jehovah had said: "I will break the yoke of the king of Babylon." Hananiah died in that very year, and you know which prophet proved reliable. (Jer. 28:1-11, 17) After Jerusalem was destroyed as Jeremiah had forewarned, Johanan and other military chiefs refused to heed God's command to stay in the land of Judah. "It is a falsehood that you are speaking," they told Jeremiah. "Our God has not sent you, saying, 'Do not enter into Egypt to reside there.'" They further defied Jehovah by taking Jeremiah and Baruch with them into Egypt.—Jer. 42:1–43:7.

*What type of individuals did Jeremiah have to deal with? What do you learn from Jeremiah's example?*

---

⁷ For years, Jeremiah was surrounded by skeptics and opponents. Reflect on his course. He could easily have resigned himself to accepting people who had little respect for God or His Word. They were all around him. What of your situation? You have likely had some dealings with people who are similar to those who were around Jeremiah. Whether they aggressively oppose you and your God or seem to be fairly pleasant people, will you choose them as friends? Would it be wise to socialize with people who do not take God's prophecies seriously? If Jeremiah were in your place, would he choose as friends people whose way of life denies the truth of God's Word or who put their trust in men?

---

7. What challenge involving faithfulness to Jehovah do you face?

(2 Chron. 19:2) God did not leave Jeremiah in doubt about the results of trusting in men rather than in God. (*Read Jeremiah 17:5, 6.*) How do you feel about that?

⁸ Some Christians have felt that they could promote their business or career by choosing to entertain worldly clients. Would pursuing such a course, though, expose such Christians to corrupt associations and dangers, such as filthy talk or heavy drinking? You can understand why many Christians who face such a decision have chosen to avoid bad associations even if it means forgoing potential profits or advancement in a worldly sense. Similarly, an employer or fellow employees might not hesitate to deal with customers dishonestly. Nevertheless, true Christians are not swayed by those around them. At times, making decisions about such matters may not be easy. We can be thankful for such examples as Jeremiah, who held to a course that left him with a good conscience and, more important, a good relationship with God.

⁹ Jeremiah's position and convictions made him an object of derision by some fellow Judeans. (Jer. 18:18) Still, he was willing to stand out as different from his contemporaries who followed "the popular course." (Jer. 8:5, 6) Jeremiah was even willing to be alone at times, 'sitting down all by himself.' He preferred that to bad company, to being friends with those who would have a negative influence on him. (*Read Jeremiah 9:4, 5; 15:17.*) What about you? Today, as in Jeremiah's day, the popular course is one of unfaithfulness to God. Jehovah's servants have long had to be cautious about their choice of friends. This is not to say that Jeremiah was without

---

8. Illustrate challenges that Christians in your area might face.
9. What danger lies in wanting to be popular?

## WHAT FRIENDS DID JEREMIAH CHOOSE?

¹⁰ With whom would Jeremiah cultivate friendship? Under Jehovah's direction, he repeatedly condemned those who were wicked, deceitful, unjust, violent, uncaring, and immoral—those who abandoned pure worship in favor of idolatry, thus committing spiritual prostitution. He urged his fellow Judeans: "Turn back, please, each one from his bad way, and make your ways and your dealings good." (Jer. 18:11) Even after Jerusalem's destruction, Jeremiah extolled God's "acts of loving-kindness," his "mercies," and his "faithfulness." (Lam. 3:22-24) Jeremiah wanted as friends only faithful servants of Jehovah.—*Read Jeremiah 17:7.*

¹¹ We are not completely in the dark about those whom Jeremiah chose as friends, or close associates. A number of men were clearly allies—Ebed-melech, Baruch, Seraiah, and the sons of Shaphan. We might ask: 'What were these men like? What association did they have with Jeremiah? In what sense were they his good friends? And how did they help Jeremiah to maintain his integrity?' Let us see, with our own situation in mind.

¹² The prophet's closest friend appears to have been Baruch, the son of Neriah. Jeremiah confidently entrusted him with the responsibilities of writing down

---

10, 11. (a) What principles determined Jeremiah's choice of friends? (b) Who were Jeremiah's friends, and what questions arise about them?

12. (a) What did Jeremiah and Baruch, depicted on page 58, have in common? (b) Who was Seraiah, and what do we know about him?

Jehovah's pronouncements as the prophet dictated them and then reading the resulting scroll, first in public and then to Judah's princes. (Jer. 36:4-8, 14, 15) Baruch shared Jeremiah's faith and conviction that what God foretold would occur. Those men had similar experiences during Judah's last 18 turbulent years. They spent much time working together on a common spiritual assignment. Both encountered difficulties and needed to hide from enemies. And both received personal encouragement from Jehovah. Baruch seems to have belonged to a prominent scribal family in Judah. The Scriptures call him "the secretary," and his brother Seraiah was an important state functionary. Like Baruch, Seraiah later worked with Jeremiah to deliver Jehovah's prophetic proclamations. (Jer. 36:32; 51:59-64) The willingness of these two sons of Neriah to work along with Jeremiah in those difficult times must have strengthened and encouraged the prophet. You too can receive strength and encouragement from those who faithfully work at your side in Jehovah's service.

*What can you learn from Jeremiah's choice of friends?*

---

[13] Ebed-melech was another outstanding ally of Jeremiah. When enraged princes cast Jeremiah into an empty cistern to die, the man who dared to defend him was a foreigner, Ebed-melech the Ethiopian. He was a eunuch, that is, an officer, in the king's house. Publicly approached Zedekiah, who was seated in the Gate of Benjamin. Ebed-melech courageously sought permission from Zedekiah to rescue Jeremiah out of the miry cistern.

---

13. As depicted on page 63, how did Ebed-melech prove himself to be a good friend to Jeremiah?

*What Friends Will You Choose?*

He took 30 men with him to do the job, which suggests that Ebed-melech might have expected physical interference from Jeremiah's enemies. (Jer. 38:7-13) We do not know just how much association Ebed-melech had with Jeremiah. Based on their friendship with Jehovah, it is logical to assume that the two were good friends. Ebed-melech knew that Jeremiah was Jehovah's prophet. He called the princes' actions "bad" and was willing to risk compromising his own position in order to do what was right. Yes, Ebed-melech was a good man. So much so that Jehovah himself assured him: "I will deliver you in [the day of Jerusalem's calamity] . . . *because you have trusted in me.*" (*Read Jeremiah 39:15-18.*) What a recommendation! Is that not the kind of friend you want?

¹⁴ Among Jeremiah's other friends were three sons and a grandson of Shaphan. They belonged to a family

---

14. What do we know about Shaphan's family and their contact with Jeremiah?

of high-ranking men, Shaphan having earlier served as the secretary of King Josiah. When Jeremiah's enemies first wanted to kill the prophet, "it was the hand of Ahikam the son of Shaphan that proved to be with Jeremiah, in order not to give him into the hand of the people." (Jer. 26:24) Ahikam had a brother named Gemariah. When Baruch read God's judgments in public, Gemariah's son Micaiah heard him and alerted his father and other princes. Concerned about Jehoiakim's reaction, they advised Jeremiah and Baruch to hide. And when the king rejected the divine message, Gemariah was among those who pleaded with the king not to burn the scroll. (Jer. 36:9-25) Jeremiah entrusted yet another of Shaphan's sons, Elasah, with a prophetic letter to the Jews exiled in Babylon. (Jer. 29:1-3) So there you have three sons and one grandson of Shaphan, all of whom supported God's prophet. Think of how Jeremiah must have appreciated such men! They were friends but not because of similar tastes in food or drink or because they liked similar entertainment or hobbies. The friendship was based on much more.

## CHOOSE YOUR FRIENDS WISELY

¹⁵ You can learn from Jeremiah's dealings with his contemporaries, bad ones and good ones. The king, many princes, false prophets, and military chiefs pressured him to change his message. Jeremiah, though, was uncompromising. His stance did little to endear him to those men, yet their friendship was not what Jeremiah was seeking. All along, his best friend was Jehovah. If hostility from certain quarters was the price to pay for faithfulness to his God, then Jeremiah was willing to pay it. (*Read Lamentations 3:52-59.*) Nonetheless, as we have seen, Jeremiah was not alone in his determination to serve Jehovah.

¹⁶ What made Ebed-melech a good friend was his faith and trust in Jehovah. This man had the courage to act decisively, saving Jeremiah's life. Baruch willingly spent much time with Jeremiah and helped him deliver Jehovah's messages. Good friends in the Christian congregation today can be just as precious as these men were. Cameron, a 20-year-old regular pioneer, appreciates the good impact that Kara, also a pioneer, had upon her. Cameron says, "Kara encouraged me to keep Jehovah first in my life, both by her example and by her words." The two sisters lived some distance apart, yet Kara would call or write Cameron on a regular basis to make sure that her friend was doing well and to have an interchange of encouragement. "She knew all about our family circumstances," recalls Cameron. "She knew what was going on with my sister and how hard it

---

15. Jeremiah set what fine example in choosing friends?
16, 17. (a) What help can a servant of Jehovah receive from a good friend? (b) In whatever country you live, where can you find the best friends?

was for me when my sister rebelled and left the truth. She was there for me through all of this, and I can't think of what I would have done without her positive influence and help. She has been an amazing support for me."

¹⁷ You can find good friends in the Christian congregation, whether they are about your same age or not. Your brothers and sisters share your faith, your values, your love for Jehovah, your hopes, and likely some of your trials. You can work side by side with them in the Christian ministry. They will be able to encourage you when you are undergoing difficulties, and you, them. They will rejoice with you when you have good times in Jehovah's service. Moreover, such friendships can last into the endless future.—Prov. 17:17; 18:24; 27:9.

¹⁸ The lesson for us from Jeremiah's choice of friends should be obvious. Bear in mind this undeniable truth: You cannot really seek companionship with people whose beliefs are in conflict with Bible teachings and still remain true to your convictions. Acting in harmony with that fact is as important today as it was in Jeremiah's time. To carry out his commission faithfully and with Jehovah's blessing, Jeremiah was willing to be different from the majority of his contemporaries. Is that not true in your case too? Jeremiah chose companions who shared his faith and who supported him in carrying out his commission. Yes, every faithful Christian today can learn from Jeremiah about choosing companions wisely!—Prov. 13:20; 22:17.

---

18. What does Jeremiah's choice of friends teach you?

***How can you apply Jeremiah's example in choosing whom you will have and whom you will not have as friends?***

## Chapter Six

# "Obey, Please, the Voice of Jehovah"

OBEDIENCE is not in style in today's world. Many do not make decisions according to even a general guideline, such as 'Do what is right.' Rather, their thinking might be summarized as 'Do what you want' or 'Do what you can get away with.' You can see this when drivers disobey traffic signals, investors violate finance statutes, and high officials break laws that they may have helped establish. Such charging ahead in "the popular course," even though it is wrong and harmful, was common in Jeremiah's day too.—Jer. 8:6.

² You realize that those desiring the favor of Almighty God must not just follow "the popular course." Significantly, Jeremiah presented a contrast between those who had "not obeyed the voice of Jehovah" and those who wanted to obey Him. (Jer. 3:25; 7:28; 26:13; 38:20; 43:4, 7) We individually should analyze where we stand in this regard. Why? Satan's attacks on the integrity of true worshippers have become particularly virulent. He is like a snake that silently lies in wait for its prey and suddenly strikes with a potentially fatal bite. Our determination to obey the voice of Jehovah helps to move us away from the fangs of that snake. But how can we strengthen our resolve to obey Jehovah? The writings of Jeremiah can help us.

---

1, 2. Those who follow "the popular course" often have what attitude, and why should you be different?

## THE ONE TO WHOM WE OWE OBEDIENCE

³ Why does Jehovah deserve our strict obedience? Jeremiah reveals one reason by calling Him "the Maker of the earth by his power, the One firmly establishing the productive land by his wisdom." (Jer. 10:12) Jehovah is the Sovereign of the universe. We should fear him above all other rulers. He has the absolute right to call on us to comply with his wise commands, which are really in our permanent best interests.—Jer. 10:6, 7.

⁴ Jehovah, however, in addition to being the Universal Ruler, is the Sustainer of life—our life. This was dramatically made plain to the Jews of Jeremiah's time. The land of Egypt depended a great deal on the waters of a river, the Nile, but the situation was different in the Promised Land. To a large extent, God's people depended on seasonal rains, often storing runoff water in underground cisterns. (Deut. 11:13-17) Only Jehovah could send rain to moisten the soil so that it would produce. On the other hand, he could also withhold the needed rain. Hence, in Jeremiah's day disobedient Jews experienced a series of devastating droughts that left their fields and vineyards parched, their wells and cisterns dry. —Jer. 3:3; 5:24; 12:4; 14:1-4, 22; 23:10.

⁵ While those Jews valued literal water, they rejected the "living water" that Jehovah freely offered them. They did this by deliberately disobeying God's Law and relying on alliances with surrounding nations. Like those who when water is scarce pour it into a cistern that is cracked and cannot hold water, the Jews

---

3. Why does Jehovah deserve our obedience?
4, 5. (a) What truth did the Jews learn during times of drought? (b) How did Judah's inhabitants waste "living water" from Jehovah? (c) How can you drink "living water" provided by God?

*Drinking the "living water" from Jehovah strengthens you to obey*

suffered the consequences. (*Read Jeremiah 2:13; 17:13.*) We certainly have reason not to bring great calamity upon ourselves by pursuing a similar course. Jehovah continues to provide us with an abundance of guidance based on his inspired Word. Obviously, that "living water" benefits us only if we regularly study it and strive to live by it.

⁶ As God's day of reckoning with Judah drew near, obedience became increasingly important. If individual Jews were to receive Jehovah's favor and protection, they had to repent and start obeying him. King Zedekiah faced this issue. He was not firm for doing what was right. When his subordinates told him they wanted to kill Jeremiah, he did not have the backbone to resist them. As we noted in the preceding chapter, the prophet survived that attempt on his life with the help of Ebed-melech and later urged Zedekiah: "Obey, please, the voice of Jehovah." (*Read Jeremiah 38:4-6, 20.*) Clearly, for his own good, the king had to make up his mind: Would he obey God?

---

6. (a) Describe King Zedekiah's attitude toward obeying Jehovah. (b) Why, do you think, was the king unwise?

*Why was it fitting for Jeremiah to urge the Jews repeatedly to obey God?*

## OBEYING JEHOVAH IS AN URGENT MATTER

⁷ Obedience is as important today as it was in Jeremiah's day. How strong is your resolve to obey Jehovah? If you were inadvertently exposed to a pornographic Internet Web site, would you keep looking at it, or would you fight any temptation and escape from that site? What if an unbeliever at work or at school asked you for a date? Would you have the strength to refuse? Would apostate literature or Internet sites intrigue you or repulse you? In these or other situations, bear in mind the words of Jeremiah 38:20.

⁸ Jehovah often sent Jeremiah to His people with exhortations, such as: "Turn back, please, each one from his bad way, and make your ways and your dealings good." (Jer. 7:3; 18:11; 25:5; *read Jeremiah 35:15.*) Comparably, Christian elders today do their best to help fellow

---

7. What are some situations in which your obedience might be tested?

8, 9. (a) Why is it wise to listen when the elders try to help you? (b) How should you view repeated counsel from the elders?

*When the elders try to help you, listen*

believers in spiritual danger. If at some time the elders offer you counsel about avoiding an unwise or wrong course, listen to them. Their goal is like that of Jeremiah.

⁹ The elders may remind you of Scriptural principles that they have already shown you. Realize that repeating counsel is never easy, but doing so becomes far more difficult if the one needing help displays an attitude like that of many of the Jews who heard Jeremiah. Try to view the elders' repeated efforts to help you as expressions of Jehovah's love. Recognize, too, that Jeremiah would not have needed to repeat his warnings if there had been an appropriate response. Yes, the way to avoid repeated counsel is to apply the counsel promptly.

## JEHOVAH'S FORGIVENESS —FREELY GIVEN BUT NOT AUTOMATIC

¹⁰ We cannot obey Jehovah perfectly in this system of things, however hard we try. So we thank him that he shows a willingness to forgive our failings. Still, he does not pardon sins automatically. Why not? Because sin is repugnant to Jehovah. (Isa. 59:2) Therefore, he wants to be sure that we are worthy of his forgiveness.

¹¹ As we have noted, many Jews in Jeremiah's time habitually disobeyed God and thus abused his patience and mercy. Could one of God's servants today develop a similar tendency? Yes, if he or she ignores Jehovah's reminders and begins practicing sin. In some cases, this has happened openly, as when someone enters into an adulterous marriage. But even if a sin is unseen by other humans, the one disobeying Jehovah is on a dangerous course. A person leading a double life might think, 'No one will find out.' Yet, the reality is that God looks

---

10. Why does Jehovah not forgive sins automatically?
11. Why is it impossible to get away with secret sins?

inside minds and hearts and can see what happens behind closed doors. (*Read Jeremiah 32:19.*) What should be done if, in fact, one has truly disobeyed God?

¹² Many Jews scorned the help Jehovah offered time and again through Jeremiah. Similarly, one guilty of serious sin today may be unrepentant, rejecting the help of the elders. In that case, the elders must follow the Scriptural direction to protect the congregation by disfellowshipping the wrongdoer. (1 Cor. 5:11-13; see the box "Living Without Law," on page 73.) But does that mean that he or she would be forever beyond hope, never able to return to Jehovah's favor? No. The Israelites were long rebellious; still God said: "Return, you renegade sons. I shall heal your renegade condition." (Jer. 3:22)\* Jehovah invites wrongdoers to return to him. Indeed, he directs them to do so.

---

\* Jehovah was here addressing the northern kingdom of Israel. Those of that ten-tribe kingdom had been in exile for some 100 years when Jeremiah delivered this message. He acknowledged that down to his day, that nation had not repented. (2 Ki. 17:16-18, 24, 34, 35) Nevertheless, individuals could return to God's favor and even return from exile.

---

12. What must the elders sometimes do to protect the congregation?

*Why is it the sensible course to seek God's forgiveness when we err?*

## OBEY JEHOVAH BY RETURNING TO HIM

¹³ To return to God, as Jeremiah indicated, a person needs to ask himself, 'What have I done?' Then, in the light of Scriptural standards, he should accept the honest answer. The unrepentant Jews of Jeremiah's time dodged

13. If someone wants to return to Jehovah, what must he recognize?

## LIVING WITHOUT LAW

What was life like among the Jews after Jerusalem's destruction? Jeremiah provides us with a partial description at Lamentations 2:9. The walls of the city were broken down, perhaps including the gates that formerly protected the city. But worse than that, there was "no law." Did Jeremiah mean that the survivors had become an uncontrollable mob? More likely he was referring to the loss of the spiritual security and comfort that the Jews had once enjoyed when faithful priests and prophets instructed them in God's Law. The false prophets who now had their attention were offering no real 'vision,' or direction, from Jehovah; what they "visioned" was worthless. —Lam. 2:14.

One who has been disfellowshipped from the Christian congregation may sense himself in a similar situation. The warm friendship he once enjoyed with his spiritual brothers and sisters is gone, as is the loving attention from the elders. And he is away from the vital spiritual instruction he had enjoyed. In the world, where there is "no law" from Jehovah, he probably feels a great sense of loss. Nevertheless, he can return to an approved condition before Jehovah and enjoy rich blessings again. (2 Cor. 2:6-10) You certainly must agree, though, that obeying Jehovah and never coming to be without law is much to be preferred.

that question. They refused to acknowledge the extent of their sins, so Jehovah did not—could not—forgive them. (*Read Jeremiah 8:6.*) In contrast, a repentant sinner recognizes that in disobeying Jehovah, he has brought reproach on God's name and on the Christian congregation. A person who is truly repentant is also deeply saddened by the harm he may have caused innocent people. He should recognize that only when he acknowledges the full effects of his bad actions will his request for forgiveness have weight with Jehovah. Still, returning to God's favor involves more.

¹⁴ A truly repentant person searches out his motives, desires, and habits. (*Read Lamentations 3:40, 41.*) He will examine areas of his life where he displays weakness, such as in his friendships with the opposite sex, his use of alcohol or tobacco, his use of the Internet, or his busi-

---

14. How does a person "return clear to Jehovah"? (Include the box "What Is Repentance?")

---

## WHAT IS REPENTANCE?

The Hebrew and Greek words related to repentance in the Bible have to do with a person's attitude; he changes his mind regarding a wrong course of action that he followed or was about to follow. Those words also describe the feelings such a person has, including regret and comfort. (2 Sam. 13:39; Job 42:6) The Bible makes clear that true repentance involves actions motivated by strong, heartfelt emotions. This kind of repentance is what Jehovah looks for in all who claim to repent of their sins.—Jer. 31:18, 19.

*'Why didn't I listen?'*

ness dealings. As a housewife scrubs even the hidden corners of her kitchen to keep her home clean and sanitary, a repentant person should work hard to clean up his thoughts and private actions. He must "return clear to Jehovah" by fulfilling God's requirements and conforming to His standards. Some Jews in Jeremiah's time returned to Jehovah "falsely." They pretended to be remorseful but never changed their hearts or lives. (Jer. 3:10) Unlike them, one whose request for forgiveness is genuine does not try to fool Jehovah and His congregation. Rather than merely wanting to save face or to regain association with relatives or others in the truth, he wants to turn his back completely on the wrongs he has committed and merit God's forgiveness and favor.

¹⁵ Prayer is a vital part of repentance. In ancient times, it was not uncommon for people to lift their hands toward heaven when praying. Today, when a truly repentant person prays, he 'raises his heart along with his

---

15. What kind of prayers does a truly repentant person offer to God?

palms to God,' as Jeremiah expressed it. (Lam. 3:41, 42) Feeling regret motivates the repentant sinner to bring his conduct in line with his plea for forgiveness. His prayers are sincere, springing from his very heart.

[16] You undoubtedly realize that a sinner who truly acknowledges his errors may have to overcome his pride. But this is a key fact: Jehovah wants sinners to come back to him. When God sees genuine contrition in a human heart, his own heart responds. He becomes "boisterous" with tender emotions because he wants to forgive all who repent of their sins, even as he did for the Israelites who returned from exile. (Jer. 31:20) How reassuring to know that God holds out peace and hope for those who obey him! (Jer. 29:11-14) They can once again have a place among God's devoted servants.

## OBEDIENCE CAN PROTECT YOU

[17] Strictly obeying Jehovah is the safe course. We can see that by the example of the Rechabites in Jeremiah's day. Over two centuries earlier, their Kenite forefather Jehonadab, who loyally took sides with Jehu, had given them a number of restrictive commands. One was against drinking wine. Jehonadab was long dead, but the Rechabites kept obeying him. As a test, Jeremiah took them to a dining room in the temple and placed wine before them, urging them to drink. They told him: "We shall drink no wine."—Jer. 35:1-10.

[18] To the Rechabites, obeying their long-dead ancestor was important. With even greater diligence, true worshippers should obey the commands of the living God.

---

16. Why is it reasonable to return to God?
17, 18. (a) Who were the Rechabites? (b) As depicted on page 77, for what are they known?

The Rechabites' resolve to obey impressed Jehovah, and it stood in stark contrast to the Jews' disobedience. God promised the Rechabites protection from the coming calamity. Applying that lesson today, is it not reasonable that those who strictly obey Jehovah are assured of his protection during the great tribulation?—*Read Jeremiah 35:19.*

*Why is repenting over serious sin an important aspect of obedience? How can obedience help one to avoid needing to repent?*

## THOSE WHO OBEY JEHOVAH ARE NOT ALONE

19 God's protective care of his people should not be viewed as limited to the past. Even now, Jehovah protects obedient ones from spiritual danger. As a high wall protected ancient cities from attack, God's law protects

---

19. What protection can God provide you if you obey him?

> ## OBEYING JEHOVAH BRINGS PROTECTION
>
> A young Witness in Spain has greatly benefited from obeying Jehovah. He writes: "In school, a girl in my class wanted me to date her. She was very pretty, yet I knew in my heart that dating someone who does not love Jehovah is dangerous.
>
> "About the same time, my classmates were pressuring me to attend an end-of-term party. When I gave them Biblical reasons why I would not, they called me names. I felt like an outcast. I mentioned the matter to an elder in my congregation. He asked me, 'Can those who do not respect your decisions and moral values become your true friends?' Those words gave me strength and helped me to resist the pressure from my classmates.
>
> "I am so glad I did. At that party, one girl was raped. That same night, three of my classmates were severely injured in a car accident because the person driving had been drinking. Had I gone to that party, I might have been in the car with them. I thank Jehovah for strengthening me to obey him in the face of peer pressure at school."

those who study it and constantly apply it. Will you stay inside the protective wall of God's moral regulations? You can be sure that it will go well with you if you do. (Jer. 7:23) Many experiences testify to that fact.—See the box "Obeying Jehovah Brings Protection."

## "Obey, Please, the Voice of Jehovah"

[20] Whether they are in your family, at your workplace or school, or among authorities where you live, opposers make serving God a challenge. You can be sure, though, that if in all cases you strictly obey Jehovah, he will support you through even the most difficult situations. Do not forget—God promised to sustain Jeremiah amid the fierce opposition he would encounter, and Jehovah did just that. (*Read Jeremiah 1:17-19.*) One of the times when God's support became evident was in the days of King Jehoiakim.

[21] Few rulers of Israel opposed God's spokesmen with fury like that of Jehoiakim. We can see this in the case of the prophet Urijah, Jeremiah's contemporary. Wicked King Jehoiakim was willing to have him pursued across international borders. When Jehovah's prophet Urijah was brought back, the king had him slain. (Jer. 26:20-23) In the fourth year of Jehoiakim's reign, Jehovah commanded Jeremiah to write down all the words He had spoken up to that time and then to read them aloud at the temple. Jehoiakim obtained Jeremiah's scroll and had a court official read it to him. As the reading proceeded, the king tore up the document and threw it into a fire piece by piece, though some of the princes urged him not to. He then sent men to arrest Jeremiah and Baruch. What happened? "Jehovah kept them concealed." (Jer. 36:1-6; *read Jeremiah 36:21-26.*) Jehovah did not allow Jehoiakim to harm those two faithful men.

[22] If Jehovah sees fit, he can also hide his modern-day

---

20, 21. (a) Of what can you be sure as you serve Jehovah? (b) How did King Jehoiakim react to God's message through Jeremiah?
22, 23. The experience of a Witness in central Asia shows you what about God's support?

servants from danger. But more often, he gives them the courage and wisdom to obey him and to continue preaching the good news. A single mother whom we shall call Gulistan has four children. She has received Jehovah's support. For a time, she was the only Witness in a wide area of central Asia where the authorities oppose the Kingdom preaching. The nearest congregation is over 250 miles away, hence Gulistan rarely has the companionship of mature Christians. Despite opposition and other problems, she preaches from house to house and finds many interested ones. According to a recent report, she was conducting Bible studies with up to 20 people and giving attention to a growing group of Jehovah's sheep.

23 Just as he helped Jeremiah and such Witnesses as Gulistan, God is ready to help you and his other obedient servants. Be resolved to obey him as Ruler rather than men. Then, opposition and other obstacles will not keep you from publicly praising the only true God before those in your territory.—Jer. 15:20, 21.

24 Real joy and satisfaction in life are unattainable if we live independently of our Creator. (Jer. 10:23) After studying what Jeremiah wrote about obedience, do you see ways in which you can let Jehovah direct your steps more fully? His commands make up the only guide for living that leads to complete happiness and success. "Obey my voice," urges Jehovah, "in order that it may go well with you."—Jer. 7:23.

24. What benefits does obedience bring you now?

***In your relationship with God, how can you apply lessons about obedience found in the book of Jeremiah?***

## Chapter Seven

# "I Will Saturate the Tired Soul"

"THE new world." On hearing those words, do you think of some of the foretold visible blessings? Perhaps a perfect body, ample healthful food, peaceful animals, or secure housing. You can likely cite Bible verses on which you base those expectations. Do not overlook, however, this blessing—good spiritual and emotional health. Without that, all other joys would soon fade.

² When having Jeremiah foretell the return of the Jews from Babylon, God gave attention to how they would *feel:* "You will yet deck yourself with your tambourines and actually go forth in the dance of those who are laughing." (*Read Jeremiah 30:18, 19; 31:4, 12-14.*) God added something that may touch you: "I will saturate the tired soul, and every languishing soul I will fill." The *NET Bible* renders God's promise: "I will fully satisfy the needs of those who are weary and fully refresh the souls of those who are faint."—Jer. 31:25.

³ What a prospect! Jehovah said that he would saturate, or fully satisfy, the one tired and discouraged. Yes, and what God promises, he does. Jeremiah's writings give us confidence that we too will be satisfied. More than that, those writings provide us with insight on

---

1. To what blessing of the new world are you particularly looking forward?
2, 3. Jeremiah's writings help us to expect what special blessing?

how, even now, we can be encouraged and optimistic. Moreover, they illustrate practical ways that we may encourage others, helping them to satisfy their tired souls.

[4] That promise was a basis for comfort to Jeremiah, and it can be the same to us. Why? Recall a point mentioned in Chapter 1 of this volume—that Jeremiah was "a man with feelings like ours," even as Elijah was. (Jas. 5:17) Think of just a few reasons why, at times, Jeremiah might have felt discouraged or even a bit depressed. As you do so, imagine how you would feel in similar situations and why circumstances that you face may discourage you.—Rom. 15:4.

[5] Jeremiah's discouragement may, in part, have come from his hometown. He grew up in Anathoth. That was a Levite city a few miles northeast of Jerusalem. The prophet would have had acquaintances and perhaps relatives in Anathoth. Jesus said that a prophet has no honor in his homeland, and this was true of Jeremiah. (John 4:44) The townspeople went beyond being disinterested in or disrespectful of Jeremiah. At one point, God said that "the men of Anathoth" were "seeking for [Jeremiah's] soul." They belligerently said: "You must not prophesy in the name of Jehovah, that you may not die at our hand." What a threat from neighbors and possibly relatives, who should have been on his side!—Jer. 1:1; 11:21.

[6] If you feel pressure from neighbors, schoolmates, workmates, or even some family members, take com-

---

4. Why can we identify with Jeremiah's feelings?
5. What may have been discouraging to Jeremiah?
6. If workmates or others oppose you, how can you benefit from Jeremiah's experience with "the men of Anathoth"?

"I Will Saturate the Tired Soul"

fort from how Jehovah dealt with Jeremiah. Back then, God said he would 'turn his attention upon' those in Anathoth who were opposing his prophet. (*Read Jeremiah 11:22, 23.*) God's assurance certainly helped Jeremiah overcome any discouragement resulting from that local opposition. Later, God's attention would—and did—result in "calamity upon the men of Anathoth." In your case, be reassured that Jehovah is observing matters, or giving them attention. (Ps. 11:4; 66:7) Your 'staying by' Bible teachings and doing what is right may yet help some opposers avoid the calamity that would otherwise befall them.—1 Tim. 4:16.

*In the book of Jeremiah, what indicates that God is interested in his people's feelings, and how might this have helped the prophet?*

## ACTS THAT COULD DISCOURAGE

⁷ Jeremiah faced far more than verbal threats from people back home. One instance centered on a notable man in Jerusalem, a priest named Pashhur.* Upon hearing a divine prophecy, "Pashhur struck Jeremiah the prophet and put him into the stocks." (Jer. 20:1, 2) Those words probably meant far more than a slap on the face. Some conclude that Pashhur had Jeremiah beaten or flogged with up to 40 stripes. (Deut. 25:3) While Jeremiah was suffering physically, people may have been jeering him and screaming abuse, even spitting on him. It did not end there. Pashhur had Jeremiah put in "stocks" overnight. The Hebrew word used suggests that the body was twisted and bent. Yes, Jeremiah was cruelly forced to suffer a painful night, probably fastened in a wooden frame.

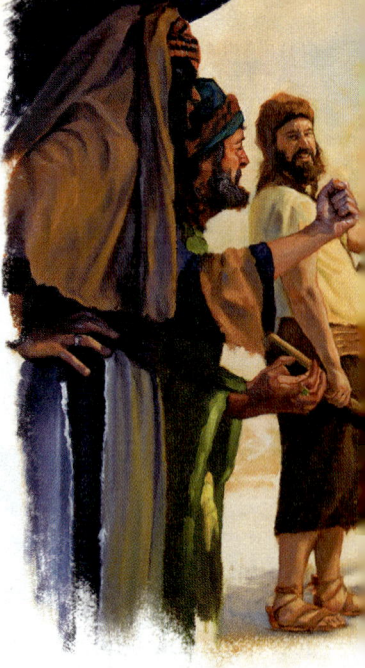

⁸ How did such treatment affect Jeremiah? He said to God: "I became an object of laughter all day long." (Jer. 20:3-7) It even crossed his mind to cease speaking out

---

* During Zedekiah's reign, there was a different Pashhur, a prince who petitioned the king to have Jeremiah killed.—Jer. 38:1-5.

7, 8. What type of abuse did Jeremiah suffer, and how did it affect him?

in God's name. You know, however, that Jeremiah could not and did not do that. Rather, the divine message he was commissioned to deliver was "like a burning fire shut up in [Jeremiah's] bones," and he had to speak for Jehovah.—*Read Jeremiah 20:8, 9.*

⁹ That account can help us if we face malicious ridicule from those we know, be they relatives, neighbors, workmates, or schoolmates. We need not be shocked if, at times, such opposition makes us feel a bit discouraged. That may also occur if we undergo physical mistreatment because we pursue true worship. The imperfect man Jeremiah was affected by such things, and do we not have human feelings like he did? Yet, we must not forget that with God's help, Jeremiah recovered his joy and confidence. The discouragement was not permanent, and it need not be so in our case.—2 Cor. 4:16-18.

---

9. Why is it helpful for us to reflect on Jeremiah's experience?

¹⁰ Sometimes Jeremiah's mood changed, even considerably. Have you too had to deal with a similar thing —perhaps feeling optimistic and positive but then feeling downcast and gloomy? Regarding the former feeling, note the words at Jeremiah 20:12, 13. (*Read.*) After what Pashhur put him through, Jeremiah rejoiced over being like one of the poor ones delivered "out of the hand of evildoers." At times, you have probably felt like exulting, desirous of singing to Jehovah, whether that was after you were somehow delivered or in response to a happy development in your life or Christian service. How fine it is to feel like that!—Acts 16:25, 26.

¹¹ Yet, because we are imperfect, our mood may change, as Jeremiah's did. After exclaiming "sing to Jehovah," he felt deep despair, perhaps with tears flowing. (*Read Jeremiah 20:14-16.*) His spirits were so low that he wondered what value there was in his having been born! In his gloomy state, he said that the man who had announced his birth was as lamentable as Sodom and Gomorrah. But here is a key issue: Did Jeremiah continue to despair? Did he give up, resigning himself to ongoing feel-

---

10. What insight does the Bible provide about Jeremiah's mood?
11. If we tend to have mood changes, what should we bear in mind about Jeremiah?

*How might opposition or ridicule affect our emotions?*

ings of discouragement? No. Instead, he must have worked to overcome his discouragement, and he succeeded. Consider what is related next, according to the arrangement of the book of Jeremiah. The other Pashhur, the prince, approached Jeremiah with an inquiry from King Zedekiah about the Babylonians besieging Jerusalem. Jeremiah rose to the occasion, boldly declaring Jehovah's judgment and what the outcome would be. (Jer. 21:1-7) Clearly, Jeremiah was continuing active as a prophet!

¹² Some of God's servants today experience mood changes. These may have a physical cause—perhaps hormonal surges or a biochemical imbalance—and a qualified physician may suggest ways to limit the extent of such mood swings. (Luke 5:31) For most of us, though, the exhilaration or gloominess that we sometimes feel is neither extreme nor abnormal. Likely, most negative feelings are a part of imperfect human life. They may result from tiredness or the loss of a loved one. If we face such situations, we can recall that Jeremiah dealt with mood changes, yet he remained in God's favor. To cope, we may need to adjust our routine to get more rest. Or we may need to give ourselves time to gain comfort after our grievous loss. However, it is vitally important that we maintain our attendance at Christian meetings and our regular share in theocratic activities. Those are keys to staying balanced and having joy in serving God.—Matt. 5:3; Rom. 12:10-12.

¹³ Whether your downheartedness is a singular, rare event or is part of a pattern of mood changes, Jeremiah's experience can speak to you. As mentioned, at times he

---

12, 13. What might we do to cope with notable changes in our mood?

felt quite down. Nevertheless, he did not let discouragement turn him away from the God whom he loved and served faithfully. When his opponents responded to his good by doing bad, he turned to Jehovah and trusted in him. (Jer. 18:19, 20, 23) Be determined to imitate Jeremiah.—Lam. 3:55-57.

*If at times you feel discouraged or gloomy, how can you apply what you find in the book of Jeremiah?*

## WILL YOU REFRESH TIRED SOULS?

¹⁴ We do well to give attention to how Jeremiah was encouraged and how he encouraged others who were 'tired souls.' (Jer. 31:25) The prophet received encouragement particularly from Jehovah. Think of how built up you would have been to hear Jehovah tell you: "As for me, here I have made you today a fortified city . . . They will be certain to fight against you, but they will not prevail against you, for 'I am with you,' is the utterance of Jehovah, 'to deliver you.'" (Jer. 1:18, 19) With good reason, Jeremiah referred to Jehovah as "my strength and my stronghold, and my place for flight in the day of distress."—Jer. 16:19.

¹⁵ It is noteworthy that Jehovah told Jeremiah: "I am with you." Do you see in that a clue as to what you can do when someone you know needs encouragement? It is one thing to realize that a Christian brother or sister or perhaps a relative has that need; it is another thing to respond effectively to that need. In many cases, the most effective course is to do what God did for Jeremiah—just

---

14. How in particular did Jeremiah receive encouragement?
15, 16. The way that Jehovah encouraged Jeremiah offers what clue as to what we can do to encourage others?

*"I Will Saturate the Tired Soul"*

be with the afflicted one. Then, at some point, offer words of encouragement, but not a torrent of words. Fewer words will likely do more good if they are words chosen to reassure and build up. What you say need not be eloquent. Use simple words that manifest interest, concern, and Christian affection. Words like that can do much good.—*Read Proverbs 25:11.*

¹⁶ Jeremiah asked: "O Jehovah, remember me and turn your attention to me." Then what? The prophet relates: "Your words were found, and I proceeded to eat them; and your word becomes to me the exultation and the rejoicing of my heart." (Jer. 15:15, 16) The one whom you want to encourage may similarly need kind attention. Granted, your words are not on the same level as those of Jehovah. You can, though, include some of God's words in what you say. Such sincere, heartfelt, Bible-based expressions can truly make the heart of the discouraged one rejoice.—*Read Jeremiah 17:7, 8.*

¹⁷ Take note that beyond receiving encouragement from God, Jeremiah encouraged others. How? At one point, King Zedekiah told Jeremiah about his fear of the Jews who allied themselves with the Babylonians. The prophet spoke encouraging words, urging the king to obey Jehovah and experience a positive outcome. (Jer. 38:19, 20) After Jerusalem fell and a mere remnant of Jews remained in the land, their military chief Johanan considered taking the people to Egypt. But first, he inquired of Jeremiah. The prophet listened to Johanan's expression and then prayed to Jehovah. Later, he conveyed Jehovah's encouraging answer, mentioning that good would come from following the divine direction

---

17. What important lesson can we draw from how Jeremiah dealt with Zedekiah and Johanan?

to remain in the land. (Jer. 42:1-12) In both cases, Jeremiah lent a hearing ear—he listened before he spoke. Listening is fundamental to encouraging others. Let the afflicted one open his heart. Listen to his concerns, his fears. When it is appropriate, offer encouraging words. You will not have a divine revelation to offer to the one needing encouragement, yet you can include positive thoughts from the Word of God, thoughts that focus on what the future holds.—Jer. 31:7-14.

[18] Neither Zedekiah nor Johanan accepted the encouraging advice Jeremiah delivered, and some today may not seem to respond to yours. Do not let that discourage you. Others did respond favorably to the encouragement Jeremiah gave them, and likely many will respond to yours. Think of the Rechabites, a group of Kenites linked to the Jews for many years. Among the commands coming down from their ancestor Jehonadab was that as alien residents, they not drink wine. When the Babylonians were attacking, Jeremiah brought the Rechabites to a dining room in the temple. At God's direction, Jeremiah set wine before them. Respectful of their ancestor and in contrast to Israel's disobedience, the Rechabites were obedient and would not drink the wine. (Jer. 35:3-10) Jeremiah conveyed to them commendation from Jehovah and His promise for their future. (*Read Jeremiah 35:14, 17-19.*) That is a pattern you can follow in offering encouragement: Honestly commend others when possible.

[19] Jeremiah also did that with Ebed-melech, an Ethiopian who evidently served as an official in the court of King Zedekiah. Judean princes had Jeremiah unjustly

---

18, 19. What pattern of encouraging others is evident in the accounts about the Rechabites and Ebed-melech?

thrown into a miry cistern and left him there to die. Ebed-melech appealed to King Zedekiah, who authorized him to save the prophet. This foreign man did so, in the face of possibly violent interference. (Jer. 38:7-13) Having likely alienated those Judean princes, Ebed-melech may have been apprehensive about his future. Jeremiah did not remain silent, just hoping that Ebed-melech would get over it. He spoke up, passing along encouraging words about God's future blessings for Ebed-melech. —Jer. 39:15-18.

[20] Truly, as we read the book of Jeremiah, we find excellent examples of how we personally can do what the apostle Paul urged our brothers in Thessalonica to do: "Keep comforting one another and building one another up . . . The undeserved kindness of our Lord Jesus Christ be with you." —1 Thess. 5:11, 28.

20. What should we want to do for our brothers, young or old?

*What lessons from Jeremiah do you plan to apply while striving to encourage tired souls?*

## CHAPTER EIGHT

# WILL YOU "KEEP LIVING," AS DID JEREMIAH?

AFTER Joshua urged the Israelites to choose whom they would serve, he said: "As for *me and my household,* we shall serve Jehovah." (Josh. 24:15) Joshua was determined to be loyal to God, and he was sure that his family too would be loyal. Much later, as Jerusalem's destruction neared, Jeremiah told King Zedekiah that if he surrendered to the Babylonians, *"you yourself and your household* will certainly keep living." (Jer. 38:17) The king's bad choice affected him, his wives, and his sons. He watched his sons be killed; then he was blinded and taken captive to Babylon.—Jer. 38:18-23; 39:6, 7.

² In each of those two italicized phrases, one person was directly involved. But his family was also mentioned. That is logical. Each adult is responsible to God. Yet, most Israelites were part of a family. The family is important for Christians too. We see that from what we read in the Bible and from what we consider at Christian meetings regarding marriage, child rearing, and respect for family members.—1 Cor. 7:36-39; 1 Tim. 5:8.

## AN UNUSUAL COMMAND

³ Jeremiah was one who did "keep living" in his day.

---

1, 2. Why is it logical to give attention to both the individual and the family?
3, 4. In what ways was Jeremiah's situation different from most, and how did he benefit?

## Will You "Keep Living," as Did Jeremiah?

He survived Jerusalem's destruction, though his personal situation was different from most. (Jer. 21:9; 40:1-4) God had told him not to marry or have offspring or share in some other common aspects of Jewish life at that time.—*Read Jeremiah 16:1-4.*

⁴ In Jeremiah's day and culture, it was normal to marry and to have children. Most Jewish men did, thus keeping the ancestral land in the tribe and family.* (Deut. 7:14) Why not Jeremiah? Because of what lay ahead, God told him not to share in normal occasions for sorrow or rejoicing. He was not to comfort mourners or to eat with them after a funeral; nor was he to take part in the levity of Jewish weddings. Such feasting and rejoicing would soon end for all. (Jer. 7:33; 16: 5-9) Jeremiah's course gave credence to his message and underscored how grave the coming judgment would be. Eventually that calamity arrived. Can you imagine the feelings of those who were reduced to cannibalism or those who saw loved ones become mere carrion? (*Read Jeremiah 14:16;* Lam. 2:20.) Thus, unmarried Jeremiah was not to be pitied. Though the 18-month siege and its carnage would wipe out families, Jeremiah would be spared the loss of a mate or children.

⁵ Could it be said, though, that Jeremiah 16:5-9 applies to us? No. Christians are urged "to comfort those in any sort of tribulation" and to "rejoice with people who rejoice." (2 Cor. 1:4; Rom. 12:15) Jesus attended a wedding and contributed to the rejoicing. Nevertheless, what lies ahead for this wicked system of things is

---

* In the Hebrew Scriptures, there is no word for "bachelor."

---

5. What bearing do the directions found at Jeremiah 16:5-9 have on Christians?

serious. Christians may even face hardships and deprivations. Jesus stressed the need to be ready to do what it takes to endure and keep faithful, as did our brothers who fled Judea in the first century. Hence, staying single, getting married, or having children merits serious thought.—*Read Matthew 24:17, 18.*

⁶ What relevance is there in God's command that Jeremiah not marry or have children? Today, some loyal Christians are unmarried or have no children. What might they learn from Jeremiah's case? And why should even Christians who are married and have children give attention to this feature of Jeremiah's life?

⁷ Consider first that Jeremiah was to remain childless. Jesus did not command his followers to abstain from having children. Yet, it is noteworthy that he pronounced "woe" on pregnant women or those nursing a baby when tribulation came on Jerusalem in 66-70 C.E. That time would be especially difficult for them, giv-

---

6. Who can benefit from reflecting on God's direction to Jeremiah?
7. That Jeremiah was to remain childless merits what consideration today?

*Will You "Keep Living," as Did Jeremiah?*

en their situation. (Matt. 24:19) We now face a greater tribulation. This should add a dimension for Christian couples who are deciding whether to have children. Do you not agree that it seems harder and harder to deal with these critical times? And couples have admitted that it has been very challenging to raise children who will "keep living" through the end of the present system. While each couple must decide if they will have children, Jeremiah's case is worth considering. But what of God's command that he not even get married?

***Jeremiah received what unusual command, and what should that move us to consider?***

## LEARN FROM JEREMIAH'S SINGLENESS

8 In telling Jeremiah not to marry, God did not establish a norm that all his servants were to follow. Marriage is good. Jehovah initiated human marriage to populate the earth and to be a source of abundant satisfaction and delight. (Prov. 5:18) Still, not all were married. There may have been some eunuchs associated with God's people while Jeremiah was prophesying.* In addition, you can be sure that there were widows and widowers. So Jeremiah was not the only true worshipper who did not have a mate. Of course, he had a reason for not marrying, and so do some Christians today.

---

* Isaiah prophetically addressed literal eunuchs in his day, who would have a limited share in Israelite worship. He foretold that by obedience eunuchs would gain "something better than sons and daughters," receiving "a name to time indefinite" in God's house. —Isa. 56:4, 5.

---

8. Why can we say that marrying is not a necessity in order to please God?

⁹ Many Christians do get married, but not all. You know that Jesus did not, and he said that some disciples would have the gift to "make room for" singleness in their mind and heart. He urged those who could to do so. (*Read Matthew 19:11, 12.*) Therefore, it would be proper to commend, not tease, one who pursues singleness so as to do more in God's service. Granted, some Christians are single, at least for a time, because of circumstances. For example, they may not have found a suitable *Christian* mate and commendably are determined to uphold God's standard to marry "only in the Lord." (1 Cor. 7: 39) And, of course, some of God's servants are widows or widowers, thus being single.\* They should never forget that God (and Jesus) have long displayed concern for such single ones.—Jer. 22:3; *read 1 Corinthians 7:8, 9.*

¹⁰ Accordingly, as Jeremiah maintained his singleness, he could draw on God for support. How? Well, recall that Jeremiah took delight in Jehovah's word. That would have been a source of strength and reassurance to Jeremiah over the decades as he focused on his God-ordained ministry. Furthermore, he carefully avoided the company of those who might ridicule him for being single. He was willing to 'sit down all by himself' rather than to be around those with such tendencies.—*Read Jeremiah 15:17.*

¹¹ Many single Christians—men and women, whether young or advanced in years—are following Jeremiah's

---

\* Others may be living alone because their mate, perhaps an unbeliever, separated from them or got a legal divorce.

---

9. What inspired counsel regarding marriage should we seriously consider?
10, 11. (a) What helped Jeremiah to make a success of singleness? (b) How do modern-day experiences bear out that those remaining unmarried can have a rewarding life?

good example. Experiences show what a great help it is to be immersed in God's service, to have a large share in meaningful spiritual activities. For example, a Witness serving with a Chinese-language congregation observes: "Pioneering gives my life direction. As a single sister, I lead a busy, active life, which helps me to avoid loneliness. I feel satisfied at the end of each day because I can see that my ministry really helps people. This gives me great joy." A pioneer aged 38 says: "I think the secret to happiness is being able to enjoy the positive aspects of whatever situation you find yourself in." An unmarried Christian in southern Europe noted frankly: "My life may not have turned out exactly as I planned, but I am happy and will continue to be so."

¹² Could it be that Jeremiah noted that his life had not turned out as he had planned while growing up? But he might wisely have seen that such is also true of many who marry and have children. A pioneer in Spain shared this insight: "I know married people who are happy and others who are unhappy. This reality convinces me that my happiness does not depend on whether I get married in the future or not." Without question, Jeremiah's experience—just one of thousands—proves that a full, rewarding, happy life is possible for one who is single. We have further confirmation from the apostle Paul, who

---

12, 13. (a) What is a realistic view of both singleness and marriage? (b) Paul's life and counsel underscore what about singleness?

> "My moments alone are among some of the most precious. I can commune with Jehovah in prayer. I can enjoy meditation and personal study without distraction. . . . Singleness has contributed not a little to my joy."—Babette

wrote: "I say to the unmarried persons and the widows, it is well for them that they remain even as I am." (1 Cor. 7:8) Paul may have been a widower. In any case, he was unmarried when he did so much in the missionary service. (1 Cor. 9:5) Is it not reasonable to conclude that his single state was an advantage? For him it meant "constant attendance upon the Lord without distraction," and thus he accomplished much good.—1 Cor. 7:35.

<sup>13</sup> Paul was inspired to add something else: "Those who [marry] will have tribulation in their flesh." God had Paul include this profound truth: "If anyone stands settled in his heart . . . to keep his own virginity, he will do well. Consequently he also that gives his virginity in marriage does well, but he that does not give it in marriage will do better." (1 Cor. 7:28, 37, 38) Jeremiah never read those words, but his course over decades proves that singleness need not stand in the way of a fulfilling life in God's service. In fact, it can contribute mightily to a very meaningful life centered on true worship. Though married, King Zedekiah did not heed Jeremiah's advice and "keep living"; whereas the unmarried prophet followed a course that allowed him to do so.

*What can you learn from Jeremiah's example of maintaining singleness over many decades?*

## REFRESH AND BE REFRESHED

<sup>14</sup> As noted earlier, most men and women in Jeremiah's day got married and were part of households. It was similar in Paul's day. Undoubtedly, most Christians with families could not engage in the ministry abroad as Paul did, but they had much to do locally. That included being a blessing to unmarried brothers or sisters. Recall that when Paul arrived in Corinth, Aquila and Priscilla welcomed him into their home and worked with him at their common trade. But there was more to it than that. The friendship that Aquila's family offered Paul would certainly have been refreshing. Think of the pleasant meals together and other occasions of warm human companionship. Did Jeremiah benefit from similar association? He was using his singleness in God's service, yet we need not think of him as a recluse. He could have enjoyed warm fellowship with families of devoted servants of God, perhaps those of Baruch, Ebed-melech, or others.—Rom. 16:3; *read Acts 18:1-3.*

<sup>15</sup> Single Christians today likewise benefit from warm companionship of the sort that Aquila's family offered Paul. If you have a family, do you make it a point to provide companionship for those who are unmarried? One sister opened her heart this way: "I've left the world and do not desire to go back. However, I still need to be cared about and loved. I pray that Jehovah will provide additional spiritual food and encouragement for us single Christians. We're not invisible, and not all of us are eager to get married. Yet, in a way it seems that we're on

---

14. The relationship between Aquila's family and Paul highlights what?
15. How can Christian families be of great help to unmarried Christians?

our own. Yes, we can always turn to Jehovah, but when we need human contact, can we talk with our spiritual family?" Thousands of single brothers and sisters can honestly respond yes. They do enjoy such human contact in their congregation. Their circle of friends extends beyond brothers and sisters their same age. Being people-oriented, they enjoy friendships with those of different ages, including older ones or the youths in local Christian families.

¹⁶ With some forethought, you can be a source of refreshment to single ones by sometimes including them in your family activities, such as your evening of Family Worship. Sharing a family meal with an unmarried

---

16. What simple things might you do to refresh unmarried Christians in your congregation?

brother or sister can mean far more than a plate of good food. Could you take the initiative to make an appointment to share in the ministry together? What about inviting a single Christian to work with your family on a Kingdom Hall maintenance project or occasionally going shopping together? And some families have invited a widow, widower, or single pioneer to join them on a trip to a convention or a vacation spot. Such association has proved to be mutually refreshing.

17 Another area to consider regarding unmarried brothers and sisters relates to the care of aged parents. In Jesus' day, some prominent Jews craftily sidestepped caring for their father and mother. They claimed that fulfilling self-imposed religious obligations came before their God-given obligations toward their parents. (Mark 7:9-13) That should not be the case in Christian families. —1 Tim. 5:3-8.

18 What, though, when aged parents have a number of Christian children? If one of the offspring is unmarried, must this person inevitably be the primary caregiver? A sister writes from Japan: "I would like to be married, but because I have the responsibility of caring for my parents, I am unable to get married. I am confident that Jehovah understands the stress of caring for parents and the pain of heart felt by single people." Could it be that she has married brothers and sisters who have decided, without consulting her, that she must be the one to provide the care? In cases like these, it is noteworthy that Jeremiah had brothers who did not treat him fairly. —*Read Jeremiah 12:6.*

---

17-19. (a) Why is loving balance needed by children in arranging to care for aged or infirm parents? (b) What practical lesson can we draw from what Jesus did regarding his mother's care?

¹⁹ Jehovah understands single people and feels for those who are experiencing trying circumstances. (Ps. 103:11-14) However, aged or infirm parents are the parents of all their children, not just of those who are unmarried. Granted, some of the children may be married and have their own offspring. However, that does not dissolve the ties of natural affection to their parents, nor does it relieve them of their Christian duty to help when care is needed. We remember that even when Jesus was near death on the stake, he sensed his duty and acted to care for his mother. (John 19:25-27) The Bible does not give detailed rules on sharing the care of elderly or infirm parents; nor does it suggest that unmarried children are automatically *more responsible* for their care. In this sensitive field, details need to be worked out with reasonableness and mutual consideration on the part of all involved, bearing in mind the example that Jesus set in caring for his mother.

²⁰ Under inspiration, Jeremiah foretold: "They will no more teach each one his companion and each one his brother, saying, 'Know Jehovah!' for they will all of them know me." (Jer. 31:34) In principle, we are already enjoying such outstanding companionship in the Christian congregation, including that with brothers and sisters who are single. Without question, all of us want to find mutual refreshment with them and to see such unmarried ones "keep living."

---

20. How do you feel about association with unmarried ones in your congregation?

**What additional steps might you take to refresh, and to be refreshed by, some unmarried brothers or sisters?**

## CHAPTER NINE

# AVOID "SEEKING GREAT THINGS FOR YOURSELF"

BARUCH, the faithful scribe of Jeremiah, had grown weary. It was the fourth year of the reign of wicked King Jehoiakim, or about 625 B.C.E. Jeremiah told the scribe to write in a roll of a book all the words that Jehovah had spoken through the prophet about Jerusalem and Judah, utterances made over the 23 years of Jeremiah's career up till then. (Jer. 25:1-3; 36:1, 2) Baruch did not read the contents of the scroll to the Jews right then. He would do that the following year. (Jer. 36:9, 10) But was something distressing Baruch?

² "Woe, now, to me," moaned Baruch, "for Jehovah has added grief to my pain! I have grown weary because of my sighing." You have likely had occasion to make utterances of weariness, whether doing so audibly or just in your heart. Whichever way Baruch did it, Jehovah was listening. The Examiner of human hearts knew what caused Baruch's troubled state, and through Jeremiah, God kindly corrected Baruch. (*Read Jeremiah 45: 1-5.*) You might wonder, though, why Baruch was feeling so weary. Was it the assignment he had received or perhaps the circumstances in which he had to perform it? His feelings really bubbled up from the heart. You see, Baruch was "seeking great things." What were

---

1, 2. (a) In the fourth year of Jehoiakim, what problem did Baruch face? (b) How did Jehovah help Baruch?

they? What assurance did Jehovah give him if he accepted God's counsel and direction? And what can we learn from Baruch's experience?

## WHAT WERE THOSE "GREAT THINGS"?

³ Baruch must have been aware of what the "great things" were. The scribe realized that God's "eyes are upon the ways of man, and all his steps he sees." (Job 34:21) The reason why Baruch felt that he had "no resting-place" while he transcribed Jeremiah's prophetic utterances was not the assignment itself. It was his own view of what seemed great—what was in his heart. Engrossed in seeking "great things" for himself, Baruch lost sight of the more important things, those pertaining to doing the divine will. (Phil. 1:10) The *New World Translation* brings out the flavor of the verb used and renders it *"keep* seeking." So it was not a momentary, passing thought. Baruch had already been seeking "great things" when Jehovah warned him to stop. Though Jeremiah's faithful secretary had been sharing in the doing of God's will, at the same time, he was yearning for "great things" for himself.

⁴ As to what Baruch's concerns were, one possibility had to do with fame and prestige. Although Baruch served as a penman for Jeremiah, he might not have been just a *personal* secretary to Jeremiah. At Jeremiah 36:32, Baruch is referred to as "the secretary." Archaeological evidence suggests that he held the position of a high royal official. In fact, the same title is used for "Elishama the secretary," who was named among Ju-

---

3. What was at the root of Baruch's spiritual problem?
4, 5. Why might Baruch's "great things" have involved fame and prestige, and why was Jehovah's warning appropriate?

dah's princes. This suggests that Baruch too had access to "the dining room of the secretary" in "the house of the king" as one of Elishama's colleagues. (Jer. 36:11, 12, 14) Baruch, then, must have been an educated official in the royal household. Seraiah, his brother, held the position of quartermaster to King Zedekiah and accompanied the king on an important mission to Babylon. (*Read Jeremiah 51:59.*) As quartermaster, Seraiah was likely in charge of supplies and lodging for the king when he was traveling, indeed a high-ranking position.

⁵ You can understand that a person accustomed to an elevated station might grow weary of recording denunciatory messages against Judah, one after another. In fact, supporting God's prophet might have put at risk Baruch's position and career. And think of the consequences if Jehovah tore down what he had built up, as we read at Jeremiah 45:4. The "great things" that Baruch had in mind—whether the gaining of additional honor in the royal court or material prosperity—might prove to be in vain. If Baruch was seeking a secure position in the doomed Jewish system of that time, God had reason to restrain him from that inclination.

⁶ On the other hand, Baruch's "great things" might have included material prosperity. The nations around Judah relied heavily on possessions and wealth. Moab trusted in her 'works and treasures.' Ammon did likewise. And Jehovah had Jeremiah describe Babylon as "abundant in treasures." (Jer. 48:1, 7; 49:1, 4; 51:1, 13) But the fact is, God condemned those nations.

⁷ Accordingly, if Baruch was seeking property and riches, you can appreciate why Jehovah warned him

---

6, 7. If Baruch's "great things" centered on material possessions, what parallels could we consider?

against that. When God 'stretched his hand out against' the Jews, their houses and fields would be turned over to their enemies. (Jer. 6:12; 20:5) Suppose you had been Baruch's contemporary living in Jerusalem. Most of your fellow countrymen—including princes, priests, and the king himself—felt that they should fight against the invading Babylonians. Yet, you learned of Jeremiah's message: "Serve the king of Babylon and keep on living." (Jer. 27:12, 17) Would having a great many possessions in the city have made it easier for you to obey the divine direction? Would your feelings about those belongings have inclined you to heed Jeremiah's warning or to follow the course of the majority? Actually, all the valuable things in Judah and Jerusalem, including those in the temple, were pillaged and taken to Babylon. So striving for material gain would have been of no use. (Jer. 27:21, 22) Is there a lesson in that?

***How did Jehovah kindly correct Baruch's inclination to seek "great things"? Why do you feel that accepting divine correction is wise?***

## "I WILL GIVE YOU YOUR SOUL AS A SPOIL"

⁸ Now consider this aspect: What would Baruch receive for obeying God's instruction? Why, his soul! That was guaranteed "as a spoil" for him. (*Read Jeremiah 45:5.*) Relatively few people were spared. Who? Those who obeyed divine direction to fall away to, that is, surrender to, the Chaldeans. (Jer. 21:9; 38:2) Some may wonder, 'Was that all they were given for their obedience?'

---

8, 9. Why would you say that Baruch's receiving his soul as a spoil was significant?

⁹ Well, imagine the state of Jerusalem during the Babylonian siege. Jerusalem was slowly seared in the heat of that siege. In contrast, Sodom was overthrown in a moment, so to speak. In a sense, Sodom's destruction might be said to have been easier to bear. (Lam. 4:6) Baruch recorded the prophecy that the inhabitants of Jerusalem were to die by the sword, by famine, or by pestilence. Then he must have seen that fulfilled. The food supply in Jerusalem hit rock bottom. What a shock to be in a city where mothers, who are by nature "compassionate," boiled and ate their own children! (Lam. 2: 20; 4:10; Jer. 19:9) Yet, Baruch survived. Yes, amid such turmoil, life itself was a spoil, like a reward to victors after a battle. Clearly, Baruch must have accepted and

followed the divine counsel not to seek "great things." And he won Jehovah's favor, as his survival testifies. —Jer. 43:5-7.

## WILL YOU SEEK "GREAT THINGS"?

¹⁰ Although Baruch was busy doing God's will, for a time he struggled with a desire for "great things." Jehovah warned him of the danger, and he was saved from spiritual disaster and from physical death. Could we, like Baruch, be tempted and perhaps overwhelmed by desires deep down in our heart, even while we are active in serving Jehovah?

¹¹ For Baruch, making a name for himself might have been a real temptation. Can you imagine him even wondering: 'Will I be able to keep my job as "the secretary"? Might I achieve an even higher office?' Now, how about us? Ask yourself, 'Do I have "ambitions," maybe ones securely guarded in my heart, to make a success of a worldly career now or in the near future?' Some younger Christians might ponder the question, 'Could the prospect of gaining prestige and financial security through scholastic achievements lure me into seeking "great things" for myself?'

¹² A brother now serving at world headquarters was 15 when he was offered a scholarship to a university. To his teachers' dismay, he did not accept that offer, preferring a career as a pioneer. Still, his love for learning never left him. He became a missionary on a remote island. There he had to learn a language spoken by a little over 10,000

---

10, 11. How does the account of Baruch relate to our day and to us personally?
12. How did one brother seek great things for Jehovah, and what is your opinion of his choice?

## Avoid "Seeking Great Things for Yourself" 109

people. There was no dictionary in that language, so he compiled a glossary on his own. He eventually mastered the language and was assigned to translate some of our Christian publications. Later, the glossary that he compiled was used as a basis for the first dictionary in that language. He once told a large audience at a district convention: "If I had accepted the university education, whatever academic works I accomplished would have been for my own glory. As it is, I have no secular qualification whatsoever. So I do not get the credit for what I have done. All the credit goes to Jehovah." (Prov. 25: 27) What do you think of the choice he made when he was 15? Over the years, he has enjoyed many privileges among God's people. In your case, how do you want to use your talents? Rather than seeking your own glory, are you determined to use them to praise Jehovah?

¹³ There is a related danger: seeking "great things" for or through ones we love and may influence. You have likely seen worldly parents maneuver matters so that their child achieves more in life than they did or becomes someone about whom they can boast. Perhaps you have heard comments like these: "I don't want him (or her) to have to work as hard as I've had to" or "I want my child to go to a university so that he'll have an easier life." Christian parents could have similar feelings. Granted, a person might say, 'I'm not seeking great things for myself.' But could he be doing so vicariously, that is, through someone else, a son or a daughter? As Baruch might have been tempted to seek prominence via his position or career, a parent might inwardly seek such through the achievements of his offspring.

---

13. Why should some parents ponder the challenge Baruch faced?

Yet, would not "the examiner of hearts" realize this, just as he did with Baruch? (Prov. 17:3) Should we not ask God to examine our innermost thoughts, as David did? (*Read Psalm 26:2; Jeremiah 17:9, 10.*) Jehovah might use various means, such as this discussion of Baruch, to alert us to the danger of seeking "great things."

*What was one possible way that Baruch was seeking "great things"? What lesson do you see in this?*

## THE TRAP OF "VALUABLE THINGS"

¹⁴ Consider the possibility that Baruch's "great things" were material riches. As noted earlier, had Baruch been deeply attached to his possessions and properties in Judah, he would probably have had a hard time obeying the divine command to surrender to the Chaldeans. You have likely seen that the rich man often relies on his "valuable things," but the Bible confirms that the protection provided by such things is "in his imagination." (Prov. 18:11) All of Jehovah's servants can benefit from reminding themselves of the balanced view of material things expressed in his Word. (*Read Proverbs 11:4.*) Yet, some may reason, 'Why not enjoy a bit of what the world has to offer?'

¹⁵ Attachment to belongings could lead a Christian to have a longing for things that are part of a passing system of things. That did not prove to be so with Jeremiah or Baruch. Years later, Jesus gave a warning to people living "when the Son of man is to be revealed." Jesus told them: "Remember the wife of Lot." It would be just as valid to urge Christians: 'Remember Jeremiah and Bar-

---

14, 15. How might riches become "great things" in our case?

uch.' (Luke 17:30-33) If we were to cultivate a strong attachment to material things, it could be hard for us to apply Jesus' words. But do not forget—Baruch took to heart God's warning and stayed alive as a result.

¹⁶ Consider the situation of the brothers in Romania during the Communist regime. While raiding the homes of Witnesses, government agents sometimes seized personal belongings, especially things that they could sell. (Lam. 5:2) Many brothers and sisters under that regime were willing to lose their possessions. Some had to leave behind their belongings and property when they were relocated; still, they kept their integrity to Jehovah. If faced with such a test, will you allow your attachment to material things to get in the way of your maintaining loyalty to God?—2 Tim. 3:11.

¹⁷ It is noteworthy that Jeremiah and Baruch received support from some of their contemporaries. Zephaniah prophesied during the reign of Josiah, when Jeremiah was serving as a prophet. What would the latter have thought about the words we find at Zephaniah 1:18? (*Read.*) And can you not picture Jeremiah sharing that

---

16. Relate a situation in which God's servants kept material things in their proper place.
17. How might some contemporaries of Jeremiah and Baruch have been of help to them?

inspired insight with Baruch? Another contemporary was Ezekiel, who was taken captive to Babylon in 617 B.C.E. Some of his activities and messages related directly to the Jews who were back in their homeland, so Jeremiah likely learned what Ezekiel said or did and vice versa. That would include the words recorded at Ezekiel 7:19. (*Read.*) Just as Jeremiah and Baruch could benefit from those inspired words, so can we. People will call out to their gods to save them on Jehovah's day. Still, neither their gods nor their wealth will save them.—Jer. 2:28.

## WILL YOU RECEIVE "YOUR SOUL AS A SPOIL"?

[18] We need to remember that what Jehovah has promised as a spoil is our "soul." Even if a few of his servants perish in the persecution that may come during "the great tribulation" when the political horns of the wild beast turn against religion, those faithful ones will not really have lost out. Their "soul" *is* guaranteed to live again to enjoy "the real life," in the new world. (Rev. 7:14, 15; 1 Tim. 6:19) We can rest assured, however, that most of God's servants who prove faithful at that time will come out of the great tribulation. You can be sure that when God brings calamity against the nations, no faithful one will be among "those slain by Jehovah." —Jer. 25:32, 33.

[19] Some may find it sobering to think that they might survive with only their "soul" as a spoil, but that actually should be no disappointment at all. Recall that while

---

18. Whose "soul" should we want to receive as a spoil, and how can we do so?
19. In what ways did considering the examples of Jeremiah and Baruch strengthen your determination to avoid seeking "great things" for yourself?

*Avoid "Seeking Great Things for Yourself"* 113

*Choose what is really valuable (Compare page 46.)*

people of Jerusalem were dying from the famine, Jehovah preserved Jeremiah alive. How? King Zedekiah put Jeremiah in custody in the Courtyard of the Guard and had him provided with "a round loaf of bread . . . daily from the street of the bakers, until all the bread was exhausted from the city." (Jer. 37:21) And Jeremiah survived! Jehovah can use whatever means he chooses to sustain his people. But sustain his people he will, for their prospect of everlasting life is guaranteed. Baruch survived the destruction of Jerusalem by not "seeking great things." Comparably, we can look forward to surviving Armageddon to praise Jehovah with our "soul" as a spoil that can be enjoyed endlessly.

*Why is it the sensible course today, not to seek "great things," but to look to receive our "soul" as a spoil?*

## Chapter Ten

# Are You Daily Asking, "Where Is Jehovah?"

JEREMIAH was in tears. He was affected both by the present condition of his people and by what God had him foretell about their future. He wished that his head were like a water source and his eyes a fountain so that he could cry without stopping. Jeremiah had reason to grieve over the condition of the nation. (Jer. 9:1-3; *read Jeremiah 8:20, 21.*) The Jews kept rejecting divine law and did not obey Jehovah's voice, thus calamity would come.—Jer. 6:19; 9:13.

² However, the people of Judah, who loved to hear the 'all-is-well' chorus of their religious leaders, were not genuinely interested in what Jehovah thought of their conduct. (Jer. 5:31; 6:14) They were like patients looking for a physician who would say soothing things but ignore serious symptoms. If you were seriously ill, would you not want an accurate diagnosis so that you could be treated in time? Spiritually speaking, the Jews in Jeremiah's day should have sought an honest appraisal of their spiritual condition. They ought to have asked: "Where is Jehovah?"—Jer. 2:6, 8.

³ For the Jews to ask, "Where is Jehovah?" would have meant seeking divine guidance when faced with deci-

---

1, 2. (a) What was the spiritual condition of the Jews of Jeremiah's day? (b) How should the Judeans have reacted to their condition?
3. (a) How could the Jews have answered the question, "Where is Jehovah?" (b) What was one way for the Jews to seek Jehovah?

sions, both major and minor. The Jews at that time did not do so. But after the desolation of Jerusalem and their return from Babylon, they were to 'seek Jehovah' and 'search for him.' By so doing, they would be able to find him and come to know his ways. (*Read Jeremiah 29:13, 14.*) How could they do that? One way was by approaching God in sincere prayer, asking for his direction. That was King David's attitude. He asked God: "Make me know your own ways, O Jehovah; teach me your own paths." (Ps. 25:4) Note the invitation that the Hearer of prayer extended through Jeremiah in the tenth year of King Zedekiah. "Call to me, and I shall answer you and readily tell you great and incomprehensible things that you have not known." (Jer. 33:3) If the king and the renegade nation called to God, He could reveal things "incomprehensible" to them, the desolation of Jerusalem and its restoration after 70 years.

[4] Another way the Jews could have sought Jehovah was by searching through history and considering how he dealt with his people. Thus they could have called to mind what had gained God's approval and what had incurred his wrath. They had Moses' writings and a number of inspired historical records as well as the annals of the kings of Israel and Judah. By meditating on those and by listening to God's true prophets, the Jews in Jeremiah's day could have grasped the answer to the question "Where is Jehovah?"

[5] A third way those Jews could have sought Jehovah was by learning through their personal experiences and those of others. Not that they had to learn everything through trial and error, but they could have benefited from considering what they themselves had done in the

---

4, 5. In what other ways could God's people have sought Jehovah?

past and how Jehovah viewed the way they had acted. If they had been observant, they could have understood how God viewed their conduct.—Prov. 17:10.

⁶ But let us bring this down to our day. Have you been regularly asking, "Where is Jehovah?" when you are making decisions and choosing your course? Some may feel that they have not been as conscientious as they should have been. If in some sense that might be true of you, do not be downhearted. Even the faithful patriarch Job struggled in this regard. When he was under pressure, he was wrapped up in himself. Elihu had to remind him of the common tendency of mankind: "No one has said, 'Where is God my Grand Maker?'" (Job 35:10) Elihu encouraged Job: "Show yourself attentive to the wonderful works of God." (Job 37:14) Job needed to observe the mighty works of Jehovah in the creation around him and in God's dealings with humans. Through his own experience, Job came to understand Jehovah's ways. After he had endured his ordeal and had seen how Jehovah handled the matter, Job said: "I talked, but I was not understanding things too wonderful

---

6. What encouragement may you find in Job's example?

## Are You Daily Asking, "Where Is Jehovah?"

for me, which I do not know. In hearsay I have heard about you, but now my own eye does see you."—Job 42: 3, 5.

⁷ As for Jeremiah himself, the prophet continued to seek Jehovah and was able to find him. Unlike his countrymen, over the decades of his faithful service, Jeremiah kept asking: "Where is Jehovah?" In what follows in this chapter, we will see from Jeremiah's example how we can seek Jehovah and find him through prayer, study, and personal experiences.—1 Chron. 28:9.

---

7. As depicted on page 116, what are we going to discuss next?

*What does it mean to ask, "Where is Jehovah?" In what ways could the Jews of Jeremiah's day have asked that?*

---

### JEREMIAH TURNED TO JEHOVAH IN PRAYER

⁸ Over the years while serving as God's mouthpiece to the nation of Judah, Jeremiah sought Jehovah through heartfelt prayers. He turned to God for support when he had to proclaim unpopular messages, when he felt that he could not continue, and when he had questions about why certain things took place. God answered him and gave direction as to how to proceed. Consider a few examples.

⁹ Once when Jeremiah was given a denunciatory message to proclaim, he felt that everyone was calling down evil upon him. So the prophet called on God to remember him. Consider his prayer, recorded at Jeremiah 15:

---

8. Under what circumstances did Jeremiah approach God in prayer?
9. (a) How did Jeremiah express himself at Jeremiah 15:15, 16, and how did Jehovah respond? (b) Why do you think it is important to express your feelings in prayer?

15, 16, in which he tells how he felt about the divine response. (*Read.*) In that prayer, Jeremiah expressed his feelings of anguish. Yet, when he found God's words and put them in his mouth, as it were, he became joyful! Jehovah helped him to appreciate the privilege of bearing the divine name and proclaiming a divine message. Jeremiah could clearly see where Jehovah was in this matter. What lesson is there in that for us?

¹⁰ On another occasion, after the priest Pashhur the son of Immer struck him, Jeremiah said that he would not speak in Jehovah's name anymore. In what way did God respond to Jeremiah's prayerful expression? (*Read Jeremiah 20:8, 9.*) The Bible does not tell us that God responded by speaking to Jeremiah from heaven. But God's word became like a burning fire shut up in his bones, and he could not help but declare it. Indeed, by honestly expressing himself before God and allowing himself to be moved by what he knew of His will, Jeremiah was motivated to follow through on what God wanted him to do.

¹¹ Jeremiah had a vexing question when he observed the wicked succeed. (*Read Jeremiah 12:1, 3.*) Though not at all questioning Jehovah's righteousness, the prophet sought a response to his "complaint." His forthrightness made it clear that he had a strong bond with God, much like that of a child with his beloved father. It was just that Jeremiah did not understand why many Jews were prospering despite being wicked. Did Jeremiah get a satisfying answer? Jehovah assured him that He would

---

10. In what way did God respond when the prophet said that he would not speak in Jehovah's name anymore?
11, 12. How did Jeremiah receive an answer to his question about the seeming success of the wicked?

## Are You Daily Asking, "Where Is Jehovah?"

uproot the wicked. (Jer. 12:14) As Jeremiah saw the outworking of the matters he took to God in prayer, his confidence in divine justice must have deepened. As a result, Jeremiah must have increasingly turned to God in prayer, expressing himself to his Father.

12 Near the end of Zedekiah's reign, when the Babylonians were laying siege to Jerusalem, Jeremiah referred to Jehovah as someone "whose eyes are opened upon all the ways of the sons of men, in order to give to each one according to his ways and according to the fruitage of his dealings." (Jer. 32:19) Jeremiah could see where Jehovah stands on the matter of justice, that God is indeed watching over what each one is doing and hearing the earnest prayers of his servants. And, correspondingly, they would see more and more evidence that He gives to "each one according to his ways and according to the fruitage of his dealings."

13 We may not feel that we have any doubt about God's justice and the wisdom of how he both accomplishes and will yet accomplish his will. Nevertheless, we can benefit from reflecting on what Jeremiah went through and bringing up in our prayers how we feel at heart. Our expressing ourselves in that way can reinforce our confidence in Jehovah, that his will is certainly going to be accomplished. Even if we do not fully understand at present why things are developing as they are, or why God's will is proceeding at the rate it is, we can express in prayer to him our confidence that he is in complete control. His will is going to take place in the way and at the pace he knows is best. This is guaranteed; we have no reason to doubt it. We will continue

---

13. Why are you confident of the outworking of God's will?

to ask, "Where is Jehovah?" in the sense of prayerfully seeking to comprehend his will and to see evidence of its outworking.—Job 36:5-7, 26.

*What assurance do you derive from Jeremiah's experiences in seeking Jehovah in prayer?*

## JEREMIAH FED HIS HEART WITH KNOWLEDGE

¹⁴ In connection with the question, "Where is Jehovah?" Jeremiah was well-aware of the need for 'knowledge of Jehovah.' (Jer. 9:24) He must have studied the history of God's people as he compiled the books now known as 1 and 2 Kings. He specifically mentioned "the book of the affairs of Solomon," "the book of the affairs of the days of the kings of Israel," and "the book of the affairs of the days of the kings of Judah." (1 Ki. 11:41; 14:19; 15:7) Accordingly, he came to understand how Jehovah had dealt with various situations. Jeremiah could see what pleased Jehovah and how He viewed people's decisions. He could also consult inspired writings available at the time, such as those by Moses, Joshua, Samuel, David, and Solomon. No doubt, he was knowledgeable about the earlier prophets as well as his contemporaries. How did Jeremiah's personal study benefit him?

¹⁵ Jeremiah recorded the account about Jezebel, the wicked wife of King Ahab of Samaria. His account included Elijah's declaration that dogs would eat up Jezebel in the plot of the land of Jezreel. (1 Ki. 21:23) And in

---

14. How do we know that Jeremiah researched the history of God's people?
15. What benefit might Jeremiah have derived from his research into Elijah's prophecy?

*Are You Daily Asking, "Where Is Jehovah?"*

harmony with what Jeremiah recorded, you know that some 14 years later, Jezebel was thrown out of a window, trampled upon by Jehu's horse, and eaten by dogs. (2 Ki. 9:31-37) Research into Elijah's prophecy and its fulfillment, even in its details, must have strengthened Jeremiah's faith in God's word. Indeed, behind his perseverance as a prophet was faith that had been built up by his study of Jehovah's past activities.

16 Let us take another example. What do you think enabled Jeremiah—despite being persecuted—to keep on warning such wicked kings as Jehoiakim and Zedekiah? A major reason was that Jehovah made Jeremiah "a fortified city and an iron pillar and copper walls" toward the kings of Judah. (Jer. 1:18, 19) But let us not overlook the fact that Jeremiah had done extensive research into the reigns of earlier kings of Judah and Israel. He had made a record of the fact that Manasseh had built "altars to all the army of the heavens in two courtyards of the house of Jehovah," had sacrificed his own son in the fire, and had shed innocent blood in very great quantity. (2 Ki. 21:1-7, 16; *read Jeremiah 15:4*.) Yet, Jeremiah must have known that when Manasseh humbled himself and kept praying to Jehovah, "He let himself be entreated," and Jehovah restored the king to his place. —*Read 2 Chronicles 33:12, 13.*

17 In his writings, Jeremiah did not mention Jehovah's mercy toward Manasseh. But Manasseh died only 15 years or so before Jeremiah embarked on his prophetic career. Hence, the prophet must have heard about what happened when the king repented of his past wickedness. Researching Manasseh's terrible

---

16, 17. Why do you think Jeremiah could persevere in warning the wicked kings of his day?

conduct and the outcome must have helped Jeremiah to see the value of urging kings, such as Zedekiah, to seek Jehovah's mercy and loving-kindness. Even a king notorious for idolatry and bloodshed could repent and be forgiven. If you had been in Jeremiah's situation, would the events involving Manasseh have encouraged you, giving you reason to persevere during the reigns of other bad kings?

## LEARNING FROM EXPERIENCE

[18] During his career as a prophet, Jeremiah certainly learned from seeing how his contemporaries acted in given situations. One was the prophet Urijah, who prophesied against Jerusalem and Judah during the reign of Jehoiakim. However, out of fear of King Jehoiakim, Urijah fled to Egypt. Thereafter, the king sent men to bring him back from Egypt, and then he had Urijah killed. (Jer. 26:20-23) Do you think Jeremiah learned a lesson from the experience of Urijah? The fact that Jeremiah kept warning the Jews of their impending doom —even doing so in the temple area—proves that he must have learned a lesson. Jeremiah maintained his courage, and Jehovah did not abandon him. God must have moved Ahikam, Shaphan's son, to protect the life of courageous Jeremiah.—Jer. 26:24.

[19] Jeremiah also learned from his own experience of being used by Jehovah to warn His people. In the fourth year of King Jehoiakim, Jehovah told Jeremiah to write down all the words that He had spoken from Josiah's day to that time. What was the reason for this divine

---

18. What could Jeremiah learn from Urijah's example, and why do you so answer?
19. Jeremiah could see what from Jehovah's persistence in sending prophets to His people?

direction? It was to encourage individuals to turn from doing bad and be forgiven. (*Read Jeremiah 36:1-3.*) Jeremiah, who got up early to give warning messages from God, even pleaded with the people to end their detestable practices. (Jer. 44:4) Is it not clear that Jeremiah must have realized from his own experience that God had sent the prophets out of compassion for His people? And would that not have engendered compassion in Jeremiah himself? (2 Chron. 36:15) You can understand, then, that when Jeremiah survived Jerusalem's destruction, he could say: "It is the acts of loving-kindness of Jehovah that we have not come to our finish, because his mercies will certainly not come to an end. They are new each morning."—Lam. 3:22, 23.

*How must Jeremiah have been affected by researching God's past dealings and meditating on what he and others had experienced? What can we learn from this?*

## DO *YOU* DAILY ASK, "WHERE IS JEHOVAH?"

[20] In the decisions that you face daily, do you make it a point to seek out what is God's will, to ask, "Where is Jehovah?" (Jer. 2:6-8) Unlike the Jews in his day, Jeremiah always looked to the Almighty for help in discerning which way he should go. Imitating Jeremiah in daily seeking Jehovah's view is undoubtedly the wise course for each of us when making a decision.

[21] The decision does not have to be regarding a major issue or a turning point in life. For example, what of the decision to go out in the field ministry on the day you planned? Perhaps you wake up and note an overcast sky, which may not be inviting. The territory scheduled for house-to-house witnessing that day may have been covered repeatedly. You may recall that some of the people turned you away with feigned politeness or with outright rudeness. At that early point in the day, could you ask in prayer, "Where is Jehovah?" Doing so might help you to think of the beauty of the message you will bear and to sense more deeply that it is God's will that you declare that message. You then might feel the word of Jehovah becoming a source of joy and exultation for you, as it was for Jeremiah. (Jer. 15:16, 20) If later during your ministry you meet someone who is very harsh or even threatening, you can again express your feelings in prayer to God. Will you? Do not forget that he can provide holy spirit so that you can respond appropriately, and your desire to speak God's message will overpower negative feelings.—Luke 12:11, 12.

---

20. How can you imitate Jeremiah in seeking Jehovah?
21. What kind of prayer might help you in connection with your ministry, such as when someone responds harshly?

*Are You Daily Asking, "Where Is Jehovah?"*

²² It is good to be aware that some prayers can be hampered, or blocked. (*Read Lamentations 3:44.*) Jehovah did not listen to the prayers of the rebellious Jews because they were 'turning their ear away from him' and persisting in a practice of lawlessness. (Prov. 28:9) The lesson must have been clear to Jeremiah, as it should be to us: If a person fails to act in harmony with his or her prayers, that will disappoint God and can result in His ceasing to hear the prayers. Surely, that is something we should seek to avoid at all costs.

²³ In addition to sincere prayer for Jehovah's direction, we need to continue in our personal study, a key means of finding out Jehovah's will. In this, we have an advantage over Jeremiah. We have the complete Bible.

---
22. Why might some prayers be blocked?
23, 24. (a) What is essential if we are to find out Jehovah's will? (b) How can you make your personal study more beneficial?

Like Jeremiah, who did deep research to compile his inspired historic account, you can rove about in the Word of God and look for divine guidance, asking, "Where is Jehovah?" By seeking to learn his will, you put trust in him, and you "will certainly become like a tree planted by the waters, that sends out its roots right by the watercourse."—*Read Jeremiah 17:5-8.*

24 As you read and meditate on the Holy Scriptures, try to discern what Jehovah wants you to do in various situations. You can look for principles that you want to remember and apply in your life. While reading historical accounts, divine commands, godly principles, and wise sayings in God's Word, consider how those passages should influence your daily decisions. In response to your asking, "Where is Jehovah?" he can reveal to you by means of his written Word how to deal with even dire situations you might face. Why, you may see in the Bible the "incomprehensible things that you have not known" or sensed in a certain light!—Jer. 33:3.

25 Additionally, you can consider experiences, your own and those of others. For instance, you may see that a few stop relying on Jehovah, as in the case of Urijah. (2 Tim. 4:10) You can learn from their course and avoid the same disastrous outcome. Call to mind often Jehovah's loving-kindness in dealing with you, remembering that Jeremiah too appreciated God's mercies and compassion. No matter how desperate your situation, do not think that the Most High does not care about you. He does, just as he cared about Jeremiah.

26 As you meditate on Jehovah's dealings with individuals today, you will realize that he is providing daily

---

25, 26. Why can experiences benefit us?

guidance in various ways. Aki, a young sister in Japan, felt that she was unworthy of being a Christian. One day when in field service with the circuit overseer's wife, Aki expressed herself: "I feel that Jehovah is about to spew me out of his mouth, but I am hanging on to his lips, asking him to give me a little more time." The circuit overseer's wife looked her in the eye and said: "I've never felt that you were a lukewarm Christian!" Later, Aki mulled over that reassuring comment. In fact, there was no real indication that Jehovah had *ever* viewed her as lukewarm. Thereafter, Aki prayed to Jehovah: "Send me wherever you wish. I will do whatever you want me to do." About that time, she visited a foreign land where there was a small Japanese group that needed someone who spoke the language and who could stay and serve with them. It so happened that Aki had been born in that land, which made it easy for her to move there and help. But where could she live? A sister whose daughter had just relocated offered a room. "It was just like pieces of a jigsaw puzzle falling into place; Jehovah was opening the way for me," Aki concluded.

27 Many brothers and sisters can relate instances in which they personally felt God's guidance, perhaps as they did Bible reading or personal study. You too may have had similar experiences. Such should strengthen your bond with Jehovah and move you to approach him in prayer even more frequently and fervently. Trust that as we daily keep asking, "Where is Jehovah?" he will show us his way.—Isa. 30:21.

---

27. Why should the question, "Where is Jehovah?" motivate you?

*How can you find an answer to the question, "Where is Jehovah?" In what ways can you search for his guidance?*

## CHAPTER ELEVEN

# "SHEPHERDS IN AGREEMENT WITH MY HEART"

HIROYASU was a small boy in Japan when his mother bought a ram and a ewe. He looked after them, and the ewe produced two lambs a year, so the flock began to grow. By the time he was 12, there were 12 or 13 sheep. "Early one morning while I was still in bed," he recalls, "I heard them bleating. I didn't go out at once. When I finally did, I saw a pack of wild dogs running away from my lambs, which had their bellies ripped open. Frantically, I searched for the mother sheep. I found her, still breathing, in a pool of blood. Only the ram survived. I was heartbroken. I should have gone to check on the flock when I first heard them. They were defenseless against the dogs."

2 In Bible times, almost everyone was familiar with the work of a shepherd. His job was to lead his flock to pastures and ensure that the animals in his care were well-fed. He also protected them against predators and searched for strays. (1 Sam. 17:34-36) The shepherd had his flock lie down to rest, undisturbed. He also assisted in the birth of lambs and then looked after these. Many Bible writers, including Jeremiah, used the figure of a shepherd as a metaphor for a man charged with the care of people, either as their ruler or as their spiritual overseer.

---

1, 2. (a) What can happen if a flock of sheep is not protected? (b) The work of a shepherd in Bible times consisted of what?

## "Shepherds in Agreement With My Heart" 129

³ Some in the Christian congregation may think of the elders as shepherds only when these men visit their brothers to help and encourage them. However, from the way Jeremiah used the terms "shepherd" and "shepherding," we can see that he applied them to all aspects of the relationship between Judah's overseers and the people. God often condemned the princes, prophets, and priests in Judah as bad shepherds because they were not seeking the best interests of the common people. (Jer. 2:8) They mistreated, misled, and neglected their "sheep" while selfishly pursuing their own interests. God's people were left in a shocking state of spiritual neglect. Jehovah pronounced "woe" on those false shepherds, and he assured his people that he would give them caring, attentive shepherds who would really protect the flock.—*Read Jeremiah 3:15; 23:1-4.*

⁴ God's promise had a major fulfillment in the Chief Shepherd of Jehovah's sheep, Jesus, who became the Head of the Christian congregation. He called himself "the fine shepherd," one who showed real compassion for those whom he led. (John 10:11-15) Today, Jehovah is using undershepherds to care for his earthly flock, both anointed brothers of the faithful and discreet slave class as well as conscientious elders of the "great crowd." (Rev. 7:9) These shepherds strive to reflect Jesus' self-sacrificing spirit. They want to feed and cherish the congregation, in imitation of Christ. Woe to any who neglect or lord it over their brothers or who adopt a harsh or arrogant attitude toward them! (Matt. 20:25-27; 1 Pet. 5:2, 3) What is Jehovah looking for in Christian

---

3. To what was Jeremiah referring when he used the terms "shepherd" and "shepherding"?
4. Who is caring for God's flock today, and with what spirit?

shepherds today? What can we learn from Jeremiah's writings about appropriate attitudes and motives for elders to have as they care for their responsibilities? Let us examine their roles as providers of help and protective care, as teachers inside and outside the congregation, and as judges.

## PROVIDING PROTECTIVE CARE

⁵ The apostle Peter called Jehovah "the shepherd and overseer of [our] souls." (1 Pet. 2:25) What attitude does God display toward his "sheep"? We find an answer by looking back to Jeremiah's day. After criticizing the bad shepherds, who scattered and neglected the flock, Jehovah said that he would "collect" his sheep, bringing them back to their pasture ground. He promised to appoint over them good shepherds, 'who would actually shepherd them' and see to it that his people were protect-

---

5-7. (a) Jehovah expects his sheep to be cared for in what way, and why? (b) How can elders show real love for their brothers, including those who have strayed?

## "Shepherds in Agreement With My Heart"

ed from rapacious enemies. (Jer. 23:3, 4) Yes, Jehovah's sheep were precious to him. His sheep today are precious too. He has paid a high price in behalf of their everlasting welfare.—1 Pet. 1:18, 19.

6 Like literal shepherds, Christian overseers should not be negligent in caring for the congregation. If you serve as an elder, are you striving to be alert to any sign of suffering on the part of your brothers, and are you willing to assist them promptly? Wise King Solomon wrote: "You ought to know positively the appearance of your flock. Set your heart to your droves." (Prov. 27:23) That verse extols the industriousness of literal shepherds; yet, in principle it may be applied to the care provided by spiritual shepherds in the congregation. If you serve as an elder, are you consciously fighting against any tendency to dominate others? The very fact that Peter mentioned "lording it over those who are God's inheritance" proves that it is distinctly possible for an elder to do so. How can you help to accomplish what is described at Jeremiah 33:12? (*Read.*) Single parents, widows, stepfamilies, the elderly, and youngsters may have special need of attention and help.

7 As a shepherd may do with literal sheep, a congregation shepherd sometimes needs to search out and help individuals who, for one reason or another, have strayed from the flock. His doing so will call for self-sacrifice and humility. He patiently spends time caring for the needs of those entrusted to his oversight. Congregation elders would do well to ask themselves frankly: 'To what extent am I striving to encourage and upbuild rather than condemn or criticize? Do I honestly want to do better?' Repeated efforts may sometimes be required to help one see things from God's perspective. If a brother or a sister

hesitates to accept Scriptural counsel (not just a personal opinion), remember the Supreme Shepherd and Overseer, Jehovah. He patiently "kept speaking" to and striving to help his wayward people. (Jer. 25:3-6) Most of God's people today do not practice bad things, but when counsel is required, an elder must offer it as did Jehovah.

8 While there was still hope that fellow Jews might return to Jehovah, Jeremiah prayed for them. He said to God: "Remember my standing before you to speak good even concerning them, to turn back your rage from them." (Jer. 18:20) You can see from these words that Jeremiah was looking for the good in his brothers, not thinking ill of them. Today, Christian overseers should imitate Jeremiah's attitude until there is clear evidence that a person has unrepentantly set his heart to do what is bad. A positive step is to commend others for the good they are doing and to pray for them and with them. —Matt. 25:21.

---

8. How may spiritual shepherds imitate Jeremiah's example?

*What promise did God make through Jeremiah regarding spiritual shepherds? How can Christian overseers provide protective care?*

---

## "THEY WILL CERTAINLY FEED YOU"

9 In harmony with what we read at Jeremiah 3:15, Christian shepherds are to "feed [others] with knowledge and insight," that is, to serve as teachers. (1 Tim. 3:2; 5:17) Jehovah promised his people that the good shepherds would do that. And he encouraged the Jews to ac-

---

9, 10. Why does being a good shepherd (congregation elder) mean being a teacher?

*"Shepherds in Agreement With My Heart"* 133

cept the corrective teaching from his prophet Jeremiah. (*Read Jeremiah 6:8.*) To be healthy, sheep need nourishment. Comparably, to remain spiritually healthy, God's people need Scriptural feeding and direction.

¹⁰ When it comes to teaching, elders have a twofold role—that of helping those who are already in the congregation and that of helping those who are not yet true Christians. As to the latter, remember: One of the chief reasons that the Christian congregation exists is to preach the good news of God's Kingdom. Accordingly, elders must be zealous evangelizers. (Jer. 1:7-10) As such, they both fulfill their own responsibility toward God and set a fine example for their brothers. If you are an elder, do you not find that regularly preaching side by side with various brothers and sisters gives you the opportunity to help them refine their teaching abilities and to refine your own? And when you zealously take the lead in evangelizing, you are giving vital encouragement, which can help the whole congregation to progress.

¹¹ What elders share in dispensing to the congregation must be based on the Bible; thus, it will be wholesome spiritual food. You can appreciate, then, that in order to be effective teachers, congregation shepherds must be zealous students of God's Word. Contrast this with what Jeremiah pointed out as to why the leaders of his people were ineffective: "The shepherds have behaved unreasoningly, and they have not looked even for Jehovah. That is why they have not acted with insight, and all their pastured animals have been scattered." (Jer. 10: 21) Those who should have been teachers were not following Scriptural principles and were not searching for

---

11, 12. An elder who wants to be a good shepherd must give attention to what?

God. Hence, they could not act with true wisdom. Jeremiah proclaimed an even stronger denunciation of the so-called prophets.—*Read Jeremiah 14:14, 15.*

¹² Unlike those false shepherds, Christian overseers study and imitate Jesus' example. Thus, they can serve as wise shepherds of the flock. It can be a challenge for them to schedule such study regularly, given the diverse demands on their time and attention. But if you serve as an elder, are you firmly convinced that your instruction can be beneficial and true, reflecting knowledge and insight, only when you base it on God's Word and direction from the faithful and discreet slave class? If you sense that you are not as involved in a personal study program as you were previously, what will you do so that you can continue to be different from the false shepherds of Jeremiah's day?

¹³ Something that made Jeremiah particularly effective as a teacher was his use of illustrations. Of course, he was instructed by Jehovah. How memorable it would have been to see him dash an earthenware pot to the ground and proclaim that in the same way, Jerusalem and its people would be smashed! (Jer. 19:1, 10, 11) Another example is that Jeremiah made and wore a wooden yoke to denote his people's suffering the severe bondage of submission to Babylon. (Jer., chaps. 27-28) The elders in your congregation have not been directed by God to carry out such dramatic actions to illustrate points. Yet, do you not appreciate it when they weave appropriate illustrations and experiences into their teaching? Truly well-thought-out and appropriate word pictures and examples can be both powerful and motivating.

---

13. What helped Jeremiah to be a good teacher, and what can Christian shepherds today learn from him?

¹⁴ How thankful we can be for the teaching done by Christian shepherds! In his day, Jeremiah saw the need for the spiritual healing of his people. He asked: "Is there no balsam in Gilead? Or is there no healer there?" (Jer. 8:22) There was *literal* balsam in Gilead, the part of Israel east of the Jordan. This aromatic plant oil was renowned for its medicinal properties, often being applied to soothe and cure wounds. However, there was no *spiritual* healing. Why? Jeremiah observed: "The prophets themselves actually prophesy in falsehood; and as for the priests, they go subduing according to their powers. And my own people have loved it that way." (Jer. 5:31) What about today? Can you not agree that there definitely is "balsam in Gilead"—yes, in your congregation? We can liken soothing balsam to the comfort that caring Christian shepherds provide by lovingly directing brothers to Scriptural principles, being upbuilding, and praying for them and with them.—Jas. 5: 14, 15.

---

14. (a) Jeremiah's reference to "balsam in Gilead" was based on what? (b) How can Christian elders promote the spiritual health of their brothers?

*What aspects of the teaching by elders in your congregation do you especially appreciate? What makes their teaching effective?*

## "THIS IS WHAT JEHOVAH HAS SAID"

[15] Imagine the joy of a literal shepherd whose hard work and long hours are rewarded by the birth of healthy lambs! He knows, though, that to thrive, those lambs will need attention. The shepherd has to ensure that they get proper nourishment. Lambs are born with long tails that may drag in manure and dirt. The shepherd wants his animals to remain clean and healthy, so he may shorten their tails, doing so skillfully to avoid causing unnecessary pain. Spiritual shepherds too give loving attention to the sheep, the members of their congregation. (John 21:16, 17) The elders are also overjoyed to see interested ones taking steps to become true Christians. Christian overseers want all the sheep, young and old, to be healthy and properly fed, so they do not let up in giving them attention, intervening when needed. This work certainly includes reminding their brothers of "what Jehovah has said," that is, what the Scriptures teach.—Jer. 2:2, 5; 7:5-7; 10:2; Titus 1:9.

[16] Jeremiah needed boldness to announce God's message. So do congregation overseers, particularly in cases where they must speak up to protect their brothers. It may be, for example, that a spiritual shepherd sees the need to intervene to prevent a 'newborn lamb' or even an older "sheep" from getting befouled by the dirt of Satan's world. The one in danger may not even be seeking counsel. Still, could a conscientious shepherd just stand by observing as a member of his flock walks into trouble? Of course not! Nor would he treat such a situation lightly, pretending that all is well when obviously it is not and could result in a fellow servant's losing his or her peace with Jehovah.—Jer. 8:11.

---

15, 16. Why do both literal and spiritual flocks need attention?

## "Shepherds in Agreement With My Heart"

<sup>17</sup> If an unwary sheep were to be induced to wander away from the flock, an alert shepherd would be quick to direct it back to safety. (*Read Jeremiah 50:6, 7.*) Similarly, on occasion an overseer might have to reason firmly but lovingly with ones who are wandering into dangerous situations. For instance, he might note that an engaged couple are spending time together without a chaperone in places where their passions might overwhelm them. A kind and understanding elder could help the couple to avoid such compromising circumstances. While being careful to avoid accusing them, he might highlight possibilities that could lead to conduct that Jehovah hates. As Jeremiah did, faithful elders condemn what God condemns. In this they imitate Jehovah, who, though not harsh, pleaded with his people through his prophet: "Do not do, *please,* this detestable sort of thing that I have hated." (Jer. 5:7; 25:4, 5; 35:15; 44:4) Do you truly appreciate the concern that loving shepherds show for the flock?

<sup>18</sup> Of course, not all those whom Jeremiah counseled listened to him. But some did. For example, when Baruch, Jeremiah's companion and secretary, needed vigorous counsel, Jeremiah willingly gave it. (Jer. 45:5) With what result? Baruch enjoyed God's favor and survived Jerusalem's destruction. Likewise today, positive results in helping fellow believers can encourage congregation elders to 'continue applying themselves' to lifesaving 'exhortation and teaching.'—1 Tim. 4:13, 16.

---

17. When and how might a shepherd have to give special attention to individual sheep?
18. What encouraging results are obtained by the efforts of spiritual shepherds?

## DISCIPLINE "TO THE PROPER DEGREE"

[19] Another role of overseers today is that of spiritual judges. On rare occasions, elders may have to deal with those who are willful sinners, wanting to lead them to repentance. Jehovah kindly but straightforwardly encouraged wrongdoers to leave their bad ways. (Jer. 4:14) If a person in the congregation will not abandon a sinful course, however, overseers must act to protect the flock from a potentially corrupting influence. As the Scriptures direct, they may have to expel the wrongdoer. Jehovah expects elders to uphold divine justice in such circumstances. Good King Josiah was exemplary in doing so. "He pleaded the legal claim of the afflicted one and the poor one." He was imitating God's love of justice. Thus, Jehovah could ask regarding Josiah's actions: "Was not that a case of knowing me?" Because Josiah executed justice and righteousness, "it went well with him." Do you not feel more secure when the elders in your congregation strive to imitate Josiah's example?—Jer. 22:11, 15, 16.

---

19, 20. Elders have what responsibility in dealing with wrongdoers?

²⁰ Be confident that Jehovah disciplines wrongdoers "to the proper degree." (Jer. 46:28) Accordingly, depending on the circumstances and the attitude manifested, the elders may have to counsel, exhort, or reprove fellow believers. And it may even be necessary to disfellowship an unrepentant wrongdoer. In that case, elders do not pray publicly for one who is expelled and is pursuing a sinful course; it would be pointless to do so.* (Jer. 7:9, 16) They will, however, imitate God by showing the disfellowshipped person how he can return to God's favor. (*Read Jeremiah 33:6-8.*) Although disfellowshipping may be painful, we can be sure that God's standards are righteous and just and the best for all.—Lam. 1:18.

²¹ When congregation shepherds identify and apply the inspired divine standards, the flock will be nourished, healthy, and well-protected. (Ps. 23:1-6) What Jeremiah tells us about attitudes and motives, both those that are appropriate and those that are not, can be useful to Christian overseers as they fulfill the serious responsibility of caring for God's sheep. Hence, each of us can ask, 'Will I continue to show appreciation for Jehovah's arrangement to teach, guide, and protect his people by supporting shepherds who "actually shepherd" the flock "with knowledge and insight"?'—Jer. 3:15; 23:4.

---

* See *The Watchtower* of December 1, 2001, pages 30-31.

---

21. What should be the condition of God's flock, and how can you contribute to such?

***In what circumstances do overseers have to act boldly? What does Jehovah expect of Christian elders when they act as judges?***

## Chapter Twelve

# "Was Not That a Case of Knowing Me?"

KING JEHOIAKIM was building a house, and it was to be grand. Plans called for spacious rooms on at least two stories. Large windows would allow sunshine to pour through as well as a constant flow of fresh air to keep the king and his family comfortable. The walls were to be paneled in aromatic cedar from Lebanon. Vermilion, an imported paint, would give the interior the rich red finish that was much-sought-after by the high and mighty of other lands.—Jer. 22:13, 14.

[2] The cost of the project was considerable. About that time, the nation's defense and the demands from Egypt for tribute had apparently depleted the treasury. (2 Ki. 23:33-35) But Jehoiakim found a way to pay for his new palace. He held back the wages of the construction workers! Jehoiakim treated them like slaves, using their sweat and toil as a contribution toward his monarchy.

[3] Through Jeremiah, God condemned Jehoiakim for his selfishness.* He reminded the king that his father, King Josiah, had shown extraordinary kindness and gen-

---

\* Regarding Jehoiakim's tragic outcome, see Chapter 4, paragraph 12, of this book.

---

1, 2. Why was it unwise for Jehoiakim to undertake his building project?
3. What contrast was there between Jehoiakim and his father, and why?

*"Was Not That a Case of Knowing Me?"*

erosity toward the working class and the poor. Josiah had even pleaded their legal cases in court. Calling Jehoiakim's attention to Josiah's consideration for the lowly, Jehovah asked: "Was not that a case of knowing me?"—*Read Jeremiah 22:15, 16.*

⁴ As conditions deteriorate in Satan's world, we need the help and protection that Jehovah gives to those who know him intimately. Thus, we should draw ever closer to God. We also need to reflect his fine qualities to have success in preaching the good news. You might wonder, though, 'How can a Christian get to know Jehovah as well as King Josiah did?'

## WHAT KNOWING GOD MEANS

⁵ Think of the ways that a good father influences the lives of his children. For example, when they observe how he shares with others who are less fortunate, they are likely moved to be openhanded. Their seeing how he treats their mother with love and respect will probably help them become considerate toward those of the opposite sex. They hear that their father is known to be fair and honest in money matters, which ought to move them to be fair and honest. Yes, by their coming to know their father's ways and qualities, such young ones will probably grow up wanting to treat others as their father does.

⁶ In like manner, a Christian who knows Jehovah as Josiah did does not simply recognize Him as Universal Sovereign. By reading the Bible, the Christian comes to know how God treats others, and then he wants to

---

4. Why should knowing Jehovah be important to you?
5, 6. (a) What influence does a good father have on his children? (b) What should be our response to knowing Jehovah's ways, in contrast with that of Jehoiakim?

imitate his heavenly Father. His love for Jehovah deepens as day by day he reflects God's likes and dislikes. In contrast, a person who ignores God's laws and reminders, thus rejecting any divine influence in his life, does not come to know the true God. He is similar to Jehoiakim, who threw into the fire Jehovah's word through Jeremiah.—*Read Jeremiah 36:21-24.*

⁷ Our success in sacred service and our prospects for life in the new world depend on our truly knowing Jehovah. (Jer. 9:24) Let us examine a few of God's qualities as revealed in Jeremiah's writings. During this consideration of God's personality, look for ways that you personally can both know him and imitate him as King Josiah did.

7. Why should you want to know Jehovah as King Josiah did?

*Why can we say that King Josiah knew Jehovah intimately? What is involved in your knowing Jehovah as Josiah did?*

## "TO TIME INDEFINITE IS HIS LOVING-KINDNESS!"

⁸ The facet of God's personality known as loving-kindness, or loyal love, defies concise definition in many languages. According to one Bible dictionary, the Hebrew term involved describes the interaction of strength, steadfastness, and love. That dictionary goes on to say: "Any understanding of the word that fails to suggest all three inevitably loses some of its richness." Thus, someone showing loving-kindness is more than a nice person. With deep concern, he tries to help others satisfy their needs, especially their spiritual needs, as best he

8. What is loving-kindness?

*Josiah and Jehoiakim—a different response to God's words*

can. His main reason for acting in such a selfless manner is his desire to please Almighty God.

⁹ The best way to grasp the essence of the Biblical expression "loving-kindness" is by studying how God treated his true worshippers down through the ages. Jehovah protected and fed the Israelites while they spent 40 years in the wilderness. In the Promised Land, God provided judges to rescue them from their enemies and to bring them back to true worship. Because Jehovah stuck with them through good times and bad during all those centuries, he could tell the nation: "With a love to time indefinite I have loved you. That is why I have drawn you with loving-kindness."—Jer. 31:3.*

---

\* *The New English Bible* renders Jehovah's words: "I have dearly loved you of old, and still I maintain my unfailing care for you."

9. What did Jehovah's treatment of Israel prove?

¹⁰ In our day, God continues to show loving-kindness in ways that directly benefit his worshippers. Consider the matter of prayer. Jehovah takes note of all sincere prayers, but he pays special attention when his dedicated servants pray to him. Even if for years we keep praying about the same chronic problems, he does not lose patience with us; nor does he tire of hearing our prayers. Once, Jehovah had Jeremiah send a message to a group of Jews already captive in Babylon. They were over 500 miles away from the temple, far from family and friends in Judah. Their being far from the temple, however, did not keep Jehovah from hearing their requests for his favor and their expressions of praise. Bearing in mind your sincere prayers, think of the comfort the Jews felt when they heard God's words, as found at Jeremiah 29:10-12.—*Read.*

10. As illustrated with the Jews in Babylon, how does Jehovah show loving-kindness in the way that he listens to prayers?

¹¹ We see another evidence of Jehovah's loving-kindness in his positive outlook. As the fall of Jerusalem approached and the city's inhabitants continued their rebellion, which amounted to a rebellion against God, what did the future hold for them? Perhaps death from famine or a Babylonian sword? At best, they might experience a long exile and death in a foreign land. Jehovah, however, held out a positive "good word" for those who repented and changed their lives. He promised to 'turn his attention' to them. He would bring them "back to this place," their homeland, from faraway Babylon. (Jer. 27:22) As a result, they would cry out: "Laud Jehovah of armies, for Jehovah is good; for to time indefinite is his loving-kindness!"—Jer. 33:10, 11.

¹² Because of his loving-kindness, Jehovah is a Source of encouragement to those who are in dire circumstances from a human standpoint. There are some today who were once part of the Christian congregation but who received needed and just discipline. They may feel overwhelmed by guilt and now hesitate to renew their association with God's people. They may wonder whether Jehovah could ever forgive them and receive them back. Almighty God has a "good word" for all such ones. They can receive kind help to make any needed changes in their thinking and practices. And what we read in the preceding paragraph can in principle apply to them—Jehovah will 'restore them to their place' among his happy people.—Jer. 31:18-20.

¹³ As the God of loving-kindness, Jehovah also loyally supports his faithful servants. In these last days of

---

11, 12. (a) What did Jehovah hold out for the people of Jerusalem? (b) What help is available for one who has received needed discipline?
13. Why should Jehovah's support of Jeremiah encourage you?

Satan's world, we have reason to trust that Jehovah will sustain and protect all who seek his Kingdom first. Bear in mind that during the last days of Jerusalem, Jeremiah depended on Jehovah for food and protection. God never let the prophet down. (Jer. 15:15; *read Lamentations 3:55-57.*) If you find yourself under great pressure of any kind, be assured that Jehovah remembers your acts of loyalty. Because of his loving-kindness, he desires to support you so that you will not 'come to your finish.' —Lam. 3:22.

*What aspect of Jehovah's loving-kindness most attracts you to him? Why do you feel that way?*

---

## "AS JEHOVAH IS ALIVE . . . IN JUSTICE!"

¹⁴ Some people spend years in prison for crimes they did not commit. There have even been cases in which

---

14. What injustices have you observed recently?

a court condemned a man to death and only after the execution did evidence of his innocence come to light. Parents in some countries are so desperate for food that they sell their children as slaves so that the family can get something to eat. How do you feel when you hear of such injustice today? How do you think Jehovah feels? The Bible makes it clear that he wants to remove all causes of suffering. He is the only One capable of doing so. Hence, the poor and innocent who suffer today can take heart. Jehovah, the God of justice, is taking steps to save them from their present distress.—Jer. 23:5, 6.

¹⁵ In Jeremiah's time, some were aware of God's superior quality of justice. For example, the prophet raised the possibility that Israel might repent of their sins and make a statement, as it were, attesting to this change of heart, saying: "As Jehovah is alive in truth, in justice and in righteousness!" (Jer. 4:1, 2) That is true because injustice has no place in Jehovah's purpose. But there are other proofs that Jehovah is a lover of justice.

¹⁶ God unquestionably keeps his word and is unhypocritical. While many humans break promises they make to others, Jehovah does not. Even the laws of nature, which he has established and from which we benefit, are unbreakable. (Jer. 31:35, 36) We can also depend on his promises and his judicial decisions, for they are always good.—*Read Lamentations 3:37, 38.*

¹⁷ When judging, Jehovah is never satisfied with the mere outward appearance of a matter. He looks beyond

---

15, 16. (a) What reality about Jehovah did Jeremiah highlight? (b) Why can you trust in God's laws and promises?
17. (a) What does Jehovah do when judging matters? (b) Why can you trust the elders' handling of problems in the congregation? (See the box "They Judge for Jehovah," on page 148.)

> ## THEY JUDGE FOR JEHOVAH
>
> Through his written Word and the Christian congregation, Jehovah has trained elders in his methods of judging. He has authorized them to represent him in handling problems in the congregation. Such brothers are imperfect, and they cannot read the heart, as Jehovah does. But they want to treat their fellow worshippers in accord with the example Almighty God sets. They pray for divine guidance and strive to apply relevant Bible principles, thus seeking to 'judge with righteousness,' as Jehovah himself does. (Jer. 11:20) Thus, you have good reason to trust the elders, "for they are keeping watch over your souls as those who will render an account."—Heb. 13:17.

the obvious to get all the facts. He also assesses the motives of those involved. Doctors can now use specialized equipment and techniques to look at a patient's heart while it is pumping, thus gaining information about its condition. Or they can examine the kidneys, which are doing the work of filtering blood. Jehovah can do much more. He examines the figurative heart and assesses a person's motives and the figurative kidneys, which reflect a person's deepest feelings. He can thus verify what moved a person to act in a certain way and how he feels about his actions. And the Almighty is not overwhelmed by the abundance of details that his close examination reveals. Better than the most insightful human judge, He uses all that information correctly and in a balanced way to determine our future.—*Read Jeremiah 12:1a; 20:12.*

¹⁸ You thus have a solid basis for trusting in Jehovah, even if at times you feel some pangs of conscience because of past mistakes. Never forget that Jehovah is not a tenacious prosecutor who looks for a reason to punish, but rather, he is a compassionate Judge who wants to help. If you have unsettled feelings over your past course or an issue involving some other person, ask Jehovah to take up "the contests," or emotional struggles, so that you can put the matter behind you.* With his help, you can see the high value God places on your continued share in sacred service.—*Read Lamentations 3:58, 59.*

¹⁹ Understandably, the God of perfect justice desires that those seeking his approval practice justice themselves. (Jer. 7:5-7; 22:3) Preaching the good news without prejudice is an important way of displaying divine justice. When you are conscientious in making return visits and conducting Bible studies, you reflect God's superior standard of justice in a truly beneficial way. How is that? He desires that all sorts of people learn about him and attain salvation. (Lam. 3:25, 26) What a privilege you have to be God's fellow worker, reflecting his justice in that lifesaving work!

---

* If a brother or a sister has engaged in conduct that clearly violates God's law, it should be brought to the attention of the congregation elders so that they can deal with the matter and provide Scriptural assistance.—Jas. 5:13-15.

---

18, 19. How can knowing God's quality of justice affect us?

***How does Jehovah's justice bring you comfort? How can you comfort others by imitating God's justice?***

## "I SHALL NOT STAY RESENTFUL TO TIME INDEFINITE"

[20] Many view the books of Jeremiah and Lamentations as mere denunciations of badness. That view ignores the heartwarming offers of forgiveness that Jehovah made to his people, as recorded in these books. He urged the Jews: "Turn back, please, each one from his bad way, and make your ways and your dealings good." Another time, Jeremiah exhorted them: "Make your ways and your dealings good, and obey the voice of Jehovah your God, and Jehovah will feel regret for the calamity that he has spoken against you." (Jer. 18:11; 26:13) In our day, Jehovah continues to forgive all who are sincerely remorseful and stop wrong practices.

[21] Yet, Jehovah goes beyond speaking about forgiveness. He acts accordingly. Jehovah used Jeremiah to exhort: "Do return, O renegade Israel . . . I shall not have my face drop angrily upon you people . . . I shall not stay resentful to time indefinite." (Jer. 3:12) God does not feel lingering anger or bitterness toward any of his people whom he has forgiven. Rather, though a wrong has been committed, Jehovah wants to repair the damaged relationship. Despite the sins a person may have committed, if that sinner truly repents and seeks God's forgiveness, Jehovah will 'bring him back' to His favor and blessing. (Jer. 15:19) That reassurance should encourage anyone now estranged from the true God to return to him. Do you not agree that Jehovah's forgiveness attracts us to him?—*Read Lamentations 5:21.*

---

20. (a) Jeremiah highlighted what aspect of God's way of dealing with people? (b) What does 'feeling regret' have to do with Jehovah's forgiveness? (See the box "How Does Jehovah 'Feel Regret'?")
21. What does Jehovah want to accomplish when he forgives a person?

## HOW DOES JEHOVAH "FEEL REGRET"?

The greatness of God's forgiveness comes into focus in his treatment of those who practiced sin but who later have a change of heart. When he observes that they turn their lives around and obey him, he comes to "feel regret." (Jer. 18:8; 26:3) In what way?

God is perfect and never errs in judgment, so it is not that he feels regret in the way that a human does when he has completely misjudged a matter. Rather, Jehovah feels regret by adjusting his dealings, responding to the change of heart he observes.

This is not just a cold rescinding of a sentence. Jehovah's feelings change toward repentant sinners. According to some scholars, the origin of the Hebrew verb translated "feel regret" in the verses cited above is thought to reflect the idea of "breathing deeply," maybe with a sigh. This may indicate that when Jehovah sees genuine remorse in a human heart, figuratively he breathes deeply, as with a sigh of relief. God can show the repentant person the loving attention enjoyed by those having His approval. That sinner may still face certain consequences, yet God is pleased with his change of heart. He softens "the calamity," or divine discipline, that otherwise might be due. (Jer. 26:13) What human judge is inclined to recognize true repentance in this way? Jehovah takes delight in doing so.—Jer. 9:24.

²² When someone offends you by thoughtless words and actions, will you imitate Jehovah? Regarding the ancient Jews, God said that he would "purify" those whom he forgave. (*Read Jeremiah 33:8.*) He is able to purify, or cleanse, in the sense of putting behind him the error of repentant ones, giving the person a new start in His service. Granted, gaining God's forgiveness does not mean that the person is purified of inherited imperfection so that he is now perfect, sinless. Still, there is a lesson for us in what God said about purifying humans. We can strive to put behind us the error, or offense, of the other person, which figuratively amounts to purifying the view of that person that we have in our heart. How so?

²³ Imagine that you received an heirloom bowl or vase as a gift. If it became soiled or stained, would your immediate response be to throw it away? Not likely. You would probably put forth effort to clean it carefully, removing any spots or dirt and perhaps eliminating the stain. You want to behold its beauty, the way it gleams in the sunlight. In like fashion, you can work hard to get

---

22, 23. As you imitate Jehovah in the matter of forgiveness, what should be your goal?

rid of any lingering rancor or feelings of annoyance toward a brother or a sister who offended you. Fight the tendency to dwell on the painful words or acts. As you succeed in putting them behind you, you purify the image and memories you have in your heart of the one whom you have forgiven. With your heart cleansed of negative thoughts toward that one, you are more open to enjoy again the close friendship that had seemed lost for good.

²⁴ We have examined just some of Jehovah's qualities and dealings that we learn about as we come to know him better. We can see that the personal benefits of knowing Jehovah intimately are a strong motivation to worship him acceptably. If we get to know Jehovah as intimately as King Josiah did, our life will be brimming with happiness, which is another aspect of God's personality.

²⁵ Knowing Jehovah to a greater extent will enrich our relationships with others. By our working to show loving-kindness, justice, and forgiveness as Jehovah does, our friendships in the Christian congregation will deepen and become more precious. Moreover, we will find ourselves more capable of teaching as we make return visits in our territory and conduct progressive Bible studies. Interested ones will feel more comfortable with the pattern of Christian living that they see in us. Hence, we will be better equipped to help them worship Jehovah acceptably, to follow "the good way."—Jer. 6:16.

---

24, 25. What benefits will you gain if you get to know Jehovah as King Josiah did?

**What message does Lamentations 5:21 convey to you?**

## CHAPTER THIRTEEN

# "JEHOVAH HAS DONE WHAT HE HAD IN MIND"

JERUSALEM lay in ruins. Smoke still rose from the fires the conquering Babylonians had lit. Jeremiah could recall the ghastly shrieks of those being slain. He had been told what was to happen, and events unfolded exactly as God had said. "Jehovah has done what he had in mind," sighed the prophet. What a tragedy Jerusalem's downfall had been!—*Read Lamentations 2:17.*

² Yes, Jeremiah saw the fulfillment of many prophecies conveyed to God's people, including ancient prophecies. Centuries earlier, Moses set before Israel the consequences of obeying or disobeying God—either "the

---

1. When Jerusalem's destruction was complete, what did Jeremiah say about Jehovah's prophecies?
2. Jeremiah saw the fulfillment of what prophecy voiced centuries earlier?

blessing" or "the malediction." Jehovah wanted the best for his people, the blessings. The maledictions resulting from disobedience, on the other hand, would be horrendous. Moses warned—and Jeremiah later repeated—that those ignoring and opposing Jehovah would even "eat the flesh of their sons and the flesh of their daughters." (Deut. 30:19, 20; Jer. 19:9; Lev. 26:29) 'Could such an awful thing actually happen?' some may have wondered. Well, during the Babylonian siege, when food was not to be found, that did occur. "The very hands of compassionate women have boiled their own children," Jeremiah reported. "They have become as bread of consolation to one during the breakdown of the daughter of my people." (Lam. 4:10) What a tragedy!

³ Of course, Jehovah's purpose in commissioning prophets like Jeremiah was not simply to announce impending doom. God wanted his people to return to a course of faithfulness. He wanted sinners to repent. Ezra pointed this out: "Jehovah the God of their forefathers kept sending against them by means of his messengers, sending again and again, because he felt *compassion* for his people and for his dwelling."—2 Chron. 36:15; *read Jeremiah 26:3, 12, 13.*

⁴ Like Jehovah, Jeremiah felt compassion for his people. You can see that from what he said before Jerusalem's fall. He was deeply perturbed by that looming disaster. This was a catastrophe that could be averted if only the people would listen to and obey the message Jeremiah bore! Try to imagine Jeremiah's emotions as he delivered God's message. "O my intestines, my intestines!" he cried. "I am in severe pains in the walls of

---

3. What was God's purpose in sending prophets to his people?
4. How did Jeremiah feel about the message he delivered?

my heart. My heart is boisterous within me. I cannot keep silent, for the sound of the horn is what my soul has heard, the alarm signal of war." (Jer. 4:19) He simply could not keep quiet about the approaching calamity.

## HOW COULD HE BE SO SURE?

[5] Why could Jeremiah be confident that what he prophesied would occur? (Jer. 1:17; 7:30; 9:22) He was a man of faith who had studied the Scriptures and knew that Jehovah is the God of true prophecy. History testified to Jehovah's ability to foretell events that seemed impossible from a human standpoint, such as the liberation of Israel from bondage in Egypt. Jeremiah was familiar with the Exodus account and with the words of one eyewitness. Joshua had reminded fellow Israelites: "You well know with all your hearts and with all your souls that not one word out of all the good words that Jehovah your God has spoken to you has failed. They have all come true for you. Not one word of them has failed." —Josh. 23:14.

[6] Why should you continue to give attention to the prophecies Jeremiah presented? First, because he had justifiable confidence in the reliability of Jehovah's words. Second, because some of God's pronouncements through Jeremiah are now being fulfilled, and you will yet see the fulfillment of others. Third, because the sheer number of announcements that Jeremiah made in God's name, as well as the vigor with which he made them, marked him as an extraordinary servant of God.

---

5. Why was Jeremiah confident about the message he preached?
6, 7. (a) Why should you be interested in Jeremiah's prophetic declarations? (b) What will help you to be confident about the message you preach?

## "Jehovah Has Done What He Had in Mind"

"Even in the company of the prophets, Jeremiah towers as a giant," notes one scholar. Jeremiah was recognized as such a powerful figure in God's dealings with His people that when Jesus was speaking, some who heard him believed that he must be Jeremiah.—Matt. 16:13, 14.

⁷ Like Jeremiah, you live at a time when crucial Bible prophecies are being fulfilled. And like Jeremiah, you need to maintain confidence in the truthfulness of God's promises. (2 Pet. 3:9-14) How can you do that? By continuing to build your trust in the absolute reliability of God's prophetic Word. To that end, in this chapter we will review a number of prophecies that Jeremiah transmitted and that he saw fulfilled. Others that we will consider were fulfilled later. And still others directly affect you now and will affect your future. Let this review strengthen your trust in Jehovah's prophetic Word so that you become even more convinced that 'he will do what he has in mind.'—Lam. 2:17.

*Why did God commission prophets? Why do you trust the prophecies about impending destruction?*

### PROPHECIES JEREMIAH STATED AND SAW FULFILLED

⁸ There are many who try to predict the future. Think of economists, politicians, spiritists, and weather forecasters. No doubt, you have seen the difficulty of making even simple predictions—what might happen in a few days or weeks—with any accuracy. But accurate prophecy is one of the Bible's hallmarks. (Isa. 41:26; 42:9) All of Jeremiah's prophecies, whether dealing with the near or the distant future, were unerring. Many of them

---

8, 9. What is one way that the Bible is an outstanding book?

concerned individuals and nations. Let us first consider a few that were fulfilled during Jeremiah's lifetime.

⁹ Who today can predict what the world scene will be in a year or two? For example, what analyst of international affairs can accurately foretell whether there will be some realignment of governmental powers? By divine inspiration, however, Jeremiah foretold the expansion of Babylon's sphere of influence. Babylon, he stated, was the "golden cup" by which Jehovah would pour out his indignation against Judah and against many nearby cities and peoples, forcing them into servitude. (Jer. 51:7) That is exactly what Jeremiah and his contemporaries witnessed.—Compare Jeremiah 25:15-29; 27:3-6; 46:13.

¹⁰ Jehovah also used Jeremiah to indicate the fate of four Judean kings. Regarding Jehoahaz, or Shallum, a son of King Josiah, God foretold that he would be exiled and would never return to Judah. (Jer. 22:11, 12) That happened. (2 Ki. 23:31-34) God proclaimed that Jehoahaz's successor, Jehoiakim, would be buried "with the burial of a he-ass." (Jer. 22:18, 19; 36:30) The Bible does not specify how he died or what was done with his corpse, but it does show that his son Jehoiachin succeeded him during the siege. Jeremiah predicted that Jehoiachin (also known as Coniah and Jeconiah) would be exiled to Babylon and would die there. (Jer. 22:24-27; 24:1) That came to pass. What of the last king, Zedekiah? Jeremiah foretold that Zedekiah would be given into the hands of enemies, who would show no compassion. (Jer. 21:1-10) What occurred? Those enemies did capture him. They slaughtered his young sons before his eyes, blinded him, and took him to Babylon, where he died. (Jer. 52:8-11) Yes, all these prophecies came true.

---

10. What did Jehovah foretell about four Judean kings?

11 We read in Jeremiah chapter 28 that during Zedekiah's reign, the false prophet Hananiah contradicted Jehovah's pronouncement through Jeremiah about Babylonian dominion over Jerusalem. Ignoring God's word, Hananiah claimed that the yoke bar of slavery that Nebuchadnezzar imposed upon Judah and other nations would be broken. However, under Jehovah's direction, Jeremiah exposed Hananiah's falsehood, reiterated that many nations would have to serve the Babylonians, and told the false prophet that he would be dead within the year. And thus it proved to be.—*Read Jeremiah 28:10-17.*

12 Of course, the central prophetic message that God gave to Jeremiah concerned the downfall of Jerusalem itself. Time and again, Jeremiah warned that the city would be overthrown unless the Jews repented of their idolatry, injustice, and violence. (Jer. 4:1; 16:18; 19:3-5, 15) Many of Jeremiah's contemporaries thought that Jehovah would never do such a thing. God's temple stood in Jerusalem. How could he allow that holy place to be destroyed? It would never happen, they thought. Yet, you know that Jehovah does not lie. He did what he had in mind.—Jer. 52:12-14.

13 God's people today find themselves in a situation comparable to that of those loyal to Jehovah in Jeremiah's day. We know that Jehovah will soon bring calamity on all who refuse to heed his warnings. Still, we can take heart from his prophetic promises, as did those Jews

---

11. Who was Hananiah, and what did Jehovah foretell about him?
12. How did most of Jeremiah's contemporaries react to his main prophetic message?
13. (a) How is our day similar to that of Jeremiah? (b) Why should promises that God made to certain individuals in Jeremiah's time interest you?

who held to pure worship in Jeremiah's time. Because of the Rechabites' faithfulness to Jehovah and to the commands of their forefather, God said that they would survive Jerusalem's fall. They did. The later mention of "Malchijah the son of Rechab," who helped repair Jerusalem during Nehemiah's governorship, may give evidence of that. (Neh. 3:14; Jer. 35:18, 19) Jehovah assured Ebed-melech that he too would survive because he trusted in God and supported Jeremiah. (Jer. 38:11-13; 39:15-18) Likewise, God promised that Jeremiah's companion Baruch would receive his "soul as a spoil." (Jer. 45:1, 5) What conclusion do you reach from the outworking of these prophecies? How do you think Jehovah will deal with you if you are faithful?—*Read 2 Peter 2:9.*

*How did the reliability of God's prophecies affect Ebed-melech, Baruch, and the Rechabites? How do you feel about such prophecies?*

*Parents: Use the examples of the Rechabites, Ebed-melech, and Baruch to build your children's faith*

## PROPHECIES FULFILLED LATER

¹⁴ God foretold that Nebuchadnezzar would conquer not only Judah but also Egypt. (Jer. 25:17-19) That must have seemed most unlikely because Egypt was so powerful, even dominating Judah. (2 Ki. 23:29-35) After Jerusalem's fall, a remnant of Jews planned to leave their land to find safety and security in Egypt. They wanted to do that despite Jehovah's having warned them not to and his saying that he would bless them if they remained in Judah. If, on the other hand, they fled to Egypt, the sword that they feared would catch up with them there. (Jer. 42:10-16; 44:30) Whether Jeremiah saw the Babylonian invasion of Egypt is not stated in his writings. What is certain is that the fulfillment of Jehovah's prophecies overtook the Israelite refugees when the Babylonians conquered Egypt early in the sixth century B.C.E.—Jer. 43:8-13.

¹⁵ Jeremiah also prophesied about the end of Egypt's conqueror, Babylon itself. A century before it occurred, Jeremiah accurately predicted the sudden fall of Babylon. How? God's prophet foretold that her protective waters would be "dried up," and her mighty men would not fight. (Jer. 50:38; 51:30) These prophecies were fulfilled in detail when the Medes and the Persians diverted the Euphrates River, waded across its bed, and then entered the city, taking the Babylonians by surprise. You would likely consider equally significant the declaration that the city would become an uninhabited wasteland. (Jer. 50:39; 51:26) To this day, the desolate condition of

---

14. Why was God's prophecy about Babylon outstanding?
15, 16. How was God's word regarding the liberation of his people realized?

once-mighty Babylon testifies to the accuracy of divine prophecy.

[16] Jehovah proclaimed through Jeremiah that the Jews would serve the Babylonians for 70 years. Then God would bring his people back to their land. (*Read Jeremiah 25:8-11; 29:10.*) Daniel had full confidence in this prophecy, and he used it to determine when "the devastations of Jerusalem" would end. (Dan. 9:2) "That Jehovah's word from the mouth of Jeremiah might be accomplished," stated Ezra, "Jehovah roused the spirit of Cyrus the king of Persia," who had conquered Babylon, to restore the Jews to their land. (Ezra 1:1-4) The returnees could thereafter exult in the peace of their homeland and restore pure worship there, as Jeremiah had foretold.—Jer. 30:8-10; 31:3, 11, 12; 32:37.

[17] Jeremiah also recorded prophecies that find fulfillment far in the future. He stated: "This is what Jehovah has said, 'In Ramah a voice is being heard, lamentation and bitter weeping; Rachel weeping over her sons. She has refused to be comforted over her sons, because they are no more.'" (Jer. 31:15) It appears that captive Jews assembled in the city of Ramah, some five miles north of Jerusalem, after its devastation in 607 B.C.E. Some prisoners may even have been executed at Ramah. That may have occasioned an initial fulfillment, as if it were Rachel weeping over the loss of her "sons." More than six centuries later, though, King Herod had infants of Bethlehem slaughtered. Gospel writer Matthew explained that Jeremiah's words foretold the bitter reaction to that massacre.—Matt. 2:16-18.

---

17. Explain how Jeremiah's words about "weeping" at Ramah may refer to two distinct occasions.

*Where are the Edomites today?*

¹⁸ Another prophecy was also fulfilled in the first century C.E. God foretold through Jeremiah that Edom was among the nations that would suffer from the Babylonian invasion. (Jer. 25:15-17, 21; 27:1-7) But the divine word went beyond that. Edom would become like Sodom and Gomorrah. You know what that meant—uninhabited for all time, ceasing to exist. (Jer. 49:7-10, 17, 18) That is exactly what happened. Where do you think the names Edom and Edomites can be found today? On any modern maps? No. They are mainly found in books of ancient and Bible history or on maps reflecting that time. Flavius Josephus recounts that the Edomites were forced to accept Judaism in the second century B.C.E. Thereafter, with the destruction of Jerusalem in 70 C.E., they ceased to exist as a distinct people.

¹⁹ As you can see, chapter after chapter of the book of Jeremiah is packed with prophecies concerning

---

18. How was God's prophecy concerning Edom fulfilled?
19. What does the book of Jeremiah reveal as to God's ability to fulfill prophecy?

individuals and nations. The majority of these prophecies have already been fulfilled. This reality alone makes the book worth your attention and study because it confirms for you something about your great God. Jehovah has done what he had in mind, and he will yet do so. (*Read Isaiah 46:9-11.*) This can strengthen your confidence in what the Bible foretells. In fact, some prophecies Jeremiah recorded have fulfillments that directly affect you and your future. Let us examine some of these in the remaining section of this chapter.

*What are some prophecies that were fulfilled after Jeremiah's death, and why are these important to you?*

## PROPHECIES THAT AFFECT YOU

20 A Bible prophecy may have more than one fulfillment. That is true of the answer Jesus gave to his disciples' question about the sign of his "presence and of the conclusion of the system of things." (Matt. 24:3) There was a fulfillment in the years 66 to 70 C.E. It is evident, however, that in certain respects that prophecy will yet be fulfilled during the "great tribulation" to come on this entire wicked system. That will be a tribulation "such as has not occurred since the world's beginning until now, no, nor will occur again." (Matt. 24:21) Similar parallels exist in the prophecies recorded by Jeremiah. Some of these had an initial fulfillment that occurred in 607 B.C.E. but a secondary fulfillment that would occur much later, as we noted in connection with "Rachel weeping over her sons." (Jer. 31:15) Indeed, some of what Jeremiah foretold refers to the time

---

20-22. Why may it be said that Bible prophecies, including some in the book of Jeremiah, have more than one fulfillment? Illustrate.

*"Jehovah Has Done What He Had in Mind"*

in which you live, and the fulfillment affects you personally.

[21] You can see that from the book of Revelation. Under inspiration, the apostle John referred back to prophecies that Jeremiah had given concerning the end of Babylon in 539 B.C.E. We find in Revelation parallels between that earlier event and what is destined to occur on a larger scale. Among the prophecies spoken by Jeremiah and fulfilled in modern times was one about the fall of a great empire—the world empire of false religion, "Babylon the Great." (Rev. 14:8; 17:1, 2, 5; Jer. 50:2; 51:8) God's people would have to "get out of her" so as not to share her fate. (Rev. 18:2, 4; Jer. 51:6) The waters of that city, symbolizing her peoples, or adherents, would "dry up."—Jer. 51:36; Rev. 16:12.

[22] Still to be fulfilled in our future is the promise that God will execute vengeance on false religion for her ill-treatment of his people. Jehovah will "pay back to her according to . . . all that she has done." (Jer. 50:29; 51:9; Rev. 18:6) And the figurative lands of false religion must become a desolate waste.—Jer. 50:39, 40.

[23] As you may have already noted, the prophecies that Jeremiah presented also have an optimistic tone. Accordingly, he foretold a restoration of true worship on earth in modern times. The release of Jewish captives from the ancient city of Babylon found a parallel in the release of God's modern-day people from Babylon the Great after the Kingdom was established in heaven. In a spiritual sense, Jehovah restored his people to pure worship, their state being marked by thanksgiving and

---

23. What spiritual restoration, foretold by Jeremiah, took place in the 20th century?

*Do not 'steal away Jehovah's words'
by concealing what is to happen*

rejoicing. He has blessed their efforts to help others come to worship him and to be richly fed spiritually. (*Read Jeremiah 30:18, 19.*) You also know from personal experience how in modern times Jehovah has fulfilled his promise to provide his people with shepherds—spiritually mature men who really care for and protect the flock.—Jer. 3:15; 23:3, 4.

²⁴ Jeremiah's words to God's ancient people balanced a promise of better things for the faithful with a warning of destruction for those not holding to their relationship with Jehovah. It is similar today. We can hardly fail to see the urgency of the warning implicit in these words: "Those slain by Jehovah will certainly come to be in that day from one end of the earth clear to the other end of the earth. They will not be bewailed, neither will

---

24. What dramatic words of Jeremiah are yet to be fulfilled?

they be gathered up or be buried. As manure on the surface of the ground they will become."—Jer. 25:33.

<sup>25</sup> Yes, like Jeremiah, we live in critical times. As in his day, people's reaction to Jehovah's message can mean life or death. God's people today are not prophets. We are not inspired to add to Jehovah's infallible words of truth found in the Bible. Still, we have been commissioned to preach the good news of the Kingdom all the days until the end of the system of things. (Matt. 28:19, 20) We certainly do not want to 'steal away Jehovah's words' by concealing from people what is about to happen. (*Read Jeremiah 23:30.*) We are determined not to take away from his words their force and effect. Many prophecies that God had Jeremiah proclaim have already been fulfilled. This assures us that those remaining to be fulfilled are absolutely trustworthy. We must tell people that God will unfailingly do 'what he has in mind and what he commanded from the days of long ago.'—Lam. 2:17.

<sup>26</sup> No consideration of Jeremiah's prophetic activity and message would be complete without giving attention to Jehovah's grand promises of "a new covenant" with his people, the laws of which he would write in their heart. (Jer. 31:31-33) This prophecy and its fulfillment, which have a direct bearing on you, are the subject of the following chapter.

---

25. God's people today have what responsibility?
26. What further prophecy remains to be considered?

***What prophecies in the book of Jeremiah have been fulfilled in modern times? How do you feel about those remaining to be fulfilled?***

## Chapter Fourteen

# You *Can* Benefit From the New Covenant

JEHOVAH gave Jeremiah a twofold commission. One part was "to uproot and to pull down and to destroy and to tear down." The other was "to build and to plant." The prophet accomplished the former by exposing the wickedness of the proud Jews, pronouncing God's judgment on them as well as on Babylon. Yet, Jeremiah's prophecies included hope for the future. He foretold the building of what God purposed to be built and the planting of what He purposed to be planted. For example, Jeremiah was fulfilling the second part of his assignment when he directed attention to the restoration of the Jews to their homeland.—Jer. 1:10; 30:17, 18.

[2] That Jeremiah proclaimed restoration did not mean that God would beforehand pamper his people or compromise his standard of justice. No, he would execute judgment on the wayward Jews. (*Read Jeremiah 16:17, 18.*) In Jeremiah's day, few in Jerusalem were "doing justice" or "seeking faithfulness," and Jehovah's patience had reached its limit. He said: "I have got tired of feeling regret." (Jer. 5:1; 15:6, 7) Those Jews had "returned to the errors of their forefathers, the first ones, who refused to obey" Jehovah's words. Moreover, they angered God by their adulterous relationship with false gods. (Jer. 11:10;

---

1. What twofold commission did Jeremiah fulfill?
2. Why did Jehovah execute judgment on his people, and to what extent?

34:18) Jehovah would correct his people, even chastise them, "to the proper degree." As a result, some individuals might come to their senses and return to him.—Jer. 30:11; 46:28.

³ God used Jeremiah to foretell something that would have much broader and long-term benefits—a new covenant. In considering Jeremiah's prophetic writings, we have ample reason to focus on this bright aspect: the new covenant. It was to replace the covenant that had been made with Israel after the Exodus, with Moses as its mediator. (*Read Jeremiah 31:31, 32.*) When instituting the Lord's Evening Meal, Jesus Christ spoke of this new covenant, so it is definitely of interest to us. (Luke 22:20) The apostle Paul referred to this covenant when writing to the Hebrews. He quoted Jeremiah's prophecy and stressed the importance of the new covenant. (Heb. 8:7-9) But what exactly *is* the new covenant? Why did it become necessary? Who are involved, and how can you personally benefit? Let us see.

## WHY THE NEW COVENANT?

⁴ To understand the new covenant, we first have to grasp the purpose of the former one, the Law covenant. It was to accomplish a number of excellent objectives for the nation that was awaiting a promised Seed, who would be a means to bless many. (Gen. 22:17, 18) When the Israelites accepted the Law covenant, they became God's "special property." Under that covenant, the tribe of Levi would provide priests for the nation. When making that national covenant between himself and Israel at Mount Sinai, Jehovah mentioned "a kingdom of priests

---

3. Why should you consider the prophecy about the new covenant?
4. What did the Law covenant accomplish?

and a holy nation" but left open when and by what means that would come about. (Ex. 19:5-8) Until it did, that covenant made it clear that the Israelites could not keep the Law in all respects. So it made their sins manifest. Hence, under the Law, the Israelites were to offer sacrifices regularly to cover their sins. Yet, there clearly was a need for something more, a perfect sacrifice that would not have to be repeated. Yes, there was a dire need for lasting forgiveness of sin.—Gal. 3:19-22.

⁵ We can thus begin to see why, even while the Law covenant was still in force, God had Jeremiah point forward to another covenant, the new covenant. Out of his love and kindness, Jehovah wanted to make permanent help available to more than one nation. Through Jeremiah, God said regarding those in this future covenant: "I shall forgive their error, and their sin I shall remember no more." (Jer. 31:34) Though that promise was given in Jeremiah's day, it holds out a wonderful prospect for all mankind. How?

⁶ We are still imperfect and often become aware of this reality. That was illustrated by a brother who was fighting against a significant personal problem. He comments: "When I relapsed, I felt terrible. I thought that I could never atone for what I had done. I found it hard to pray. I would start by saying, 'Jehovah, I don't know whether you are going to hear this prayer, but . . .'" Some who have had such a relapse or have committed a sin have felt as if "a cloud mass" were blocking their prayers from reaching God. (Lam. 3:44) Others have been haunted by memories of past wrongdoing, years

---

5. Why did Jehovah foretell the new covenant?
6, 7. (a) How do some feel about their sinfulness? (b) Why can considering the new covenant encourage you?

*You Can Benefit From the New Covenant*

after the incident. Even otherwise exemplary Christians may say things that they later regret.—Jas. 3:5-10.

⁷ None of us should feel that we could never stray into inappropriate conduct. (1 Cor. 10:12) Even the apostle Paul realized that he erred. (*Read Romans 7:21-25.*) In this connection, the new covenant should come to mind. God promised that one key aspect of the new covenant would be his remembering sins no more. What an incomparable benefit! Foretelling that must have truly moved Jeremiah, and we can similarly be moved as we learn more about the new covenant and see how we can benefit from it.

*Why did God conclude a new covenant?*

## WHAT IS THE NEW COVENANT?

⁸ As you come to know Jehovah better, you increasingly realize how kind and merciful he is to imperfect humans. (Ps. 103:13, 14) In foretelling the new covenant, Jeremiah highlighted that Jehovah would "forgive their error" and remember sin no more. (Jer. 31:34) You can imagine that Jeremiah might have wondered how God would accomplish that forgiveness. At least he could understand that in speaking of a new *covenant,* God meant that there would be an agreement, or contract, between Him and humans. Somehow, by means of that covenant, Jehovah would accomplish what he inspired Jeremiah to outline, including forgiveness. More details would have to await God's further revealing of his purpose, including what the Messiah would do.

⁹ You may have seen parents who spoil their children,

---

8, 9. What did it cost Jehovah to make forgiveness of sin possible?

not disciplining them. Would you expect Jehovah to be like that? Not at all! This is clear from the way the new covenant took effect. Instead of just canceling sins, God scrupulously met his own standard of justice by providing the legal basis for forgiving sins, doing so at great cost to himself. You can gain insight into this by noting what Paul wrote when discussing the new covenant. (*Read Hebrews 9:15, 22, 28.*) Paul mentioned "release by ransom" and said that "unless blood is poured out no forgiveness takes place." In the case of the new covenant, this did not mean the sacrificial blood of bulls or goats as offered under the Law. No, the new covenant was made operative by Jesus' blood. Based on that perfect sacrifice, Jehovah could 'forgive error and sin' lastingly. (Acts 2:38; 3:19) But who would be in this new covenant and gain that forgiveness? Not the Jewish nation. Jesus said that God would reject the Jews, those who offered animal sacrifices under the Law, and He would turn to another nation. (Matt. 21:43; Acts 3:13-15) That proved to be "the Israel of God," composed of Christians anointed with holy spirit. In basic terms, the

## You Can Benefit From the New Covenant

Law covenant was between God and natural Israel, while the new covenant is between Jehovah God and spiritual Israel, with Jesus as its Mediator.—Gal. 6:16; Rom. 9:6.

[10] Jeremiah depicted the coming One, the Messiah, as the "sprout" for David. That is fitting. Even while Jeremiah was serving as a prophet, David's royal family tree was cut down. However, the stump was not dead. In time, Jesus was born in the line of King David. He could be called "Jehovah Is Our Righteousness," highlighting God's deep concern for that quality. (*Read Jeremiah 23: 5, 6.*) Jehovah allowed his only-begotten Son to experience suffering on earth and to die. Then Jehovah—in harmony with justice—could apply the value of the ransom sacrifice of the "sprout" for David as a basis for forgiveness. (Jer. 33:15) This opened the way for some humans to be declared "righteous for life" and anointed with holy spirit, becoming parties to the new covenant. As further evidence of God's concern for righteousness, others who are not directly in that covenant can and do benefit from it, as we will see.—Rom. 5:18.

[11] Would you like to know other distinctive aspects of the new covenant? One major difference between it and the Mosaic Law covenant is what they were written on. (*Read Jeremiah 31:33.*) The Ten Commandments of the Law covenant were written on stone tablets, which eventually disappeared. In contrast, Jeremiah prophesied that the law of the new covenant would be written in human hearts, and it would endure. Those who are parties to the new covenant, anointed Christians, truly appreciate this

---

10. (a) Who is the "sprout" for David? (b) How can humans benefit from the "sprout"?
11. (a) On what is the law of the new covenant written? (b) Why are the "other sheep" interested in the law of the new covenant?

*"The law of the Christ" moves one to serve Jehovah willingly*

law. What of those who are not directly in the new covenant, the "other sheep," who hope to live forever on earth? (John 10:16) These too delight in God's law. In a sense, they are like the alien residents in Israel, who accepted and benefited from the Mosaic Law. —Lev. 24:22; Num. 15:15.

¹² How would you reply if asked, 'What is this law that is inscribed in the heart of anointed Christians?' Well, this law is also called "the law of the Christ." It was first given to spiritual Israelites, those in the new covenant. (Gal. 6:2; Rom. 2:28, 29) You could sum up "the law of the Christ" in one word: love. (Matt. 22:36-39) How do those of the anointed get this law written in their heart? Key ways are by their studying God's Word and approaching Jehovah in prayer. Accordingly, those aspects of true worship should be regular features of the lives of all true Christians, even those who are not in the new covenant but who want to benefit from it.

¹³ "The law of the Christ" is referred to as "the perfect law that belongs to freedom" and "the law of a free peo-

---

12, 13. (a) What is the law of the new covenant? (b) Under "the law of the Christ," why would you not feel coerced into serving God?

ple." (Jas. 1:25; 2:12) Many were born under the Mosaic Law, but no one is born into the new covenant or under the law of the Christ. None who become obedient to the law of the Christ are coerced into serving God. Rather, they are delighted to know that God's law can be written in hearts and that lasting benefits of the covenant that Jeremiah foretold are available to humans today.

*How did God make forgiveness possible through the new covenant? How can you learn about the law that is written in hearts?*

## BENEFICIARIES OF THE NEW COVENANT

¹⁴ Upon learning that the 144,000 are in the new covenant, some may have thought that only these benefit from it. Perhaps they thought so because only anointed ones are to partake of the emblems at the annual Memorial of Christ's death, where the wine represents the "blood of the covenant." (Mark 14:24) Recall, though, that those in the new covenant are to be associates with Jesus as the "seed" of Abraham, by means of which all nations will be blessed. (Gal. 3:8, 9, 29; Gen. 12:3) Somehow, through the new covenant, Jehovah will fulfill his promise to bless all mankind through Abraham's "seed."

¹⁵ Jesus Christ, the primary part of the seed of Abraham, serves as High Priest, and he provided the perfect sacrifice that makes possible forgiveness of error and sin. (*Read Hebrews 2:17, 18.*) Yet, God long ago pointed forward to "a kingdom of priests and a holy nation." (Ex. 19:6) In natural Israel the priests were from one tribe,

---

14. Who clearly benefit from the new covenant?
15. What role are the anointed foretold to have?

and the kings were from a different tribe. So how would this promised nation of king-priests come about? The apostle Peter directed his first letter to ones who were sanctified by the spirit. (1 Pet. 1:1, 2) He referred to such ones as "a royal priesthood, a holy nation, a people for special possession." (1 Pet. 2:9) Anointed Christians in the new covenant will thus serve as underpriests. Think of what that means! We daily struggle under the influence of sin, which still 'rules as king.' Those serving as underpriests will have had a similar experience. (Rom. 5:21) They will be aware of how it feels to make mistakes and grapple with guilt. So along with Christ, they will be able to sympathize with us as we overcome sinful tendencies.

16 At Revelation 7:9, 14, the "great crowd" are seen "dressed in white robes," which implies a clean standing with God. To be in line to survive "the great tribulation," that great crowd is now being formed. Hence, even now these gain a certain righteous standing before God. They are being declared righteous as Jehovah's friends. (Rom. 4:2, 3; Jas. 2:23) What a benefit that is! If you are part of the great crowd, you can be sure that God is willing to work with you as you strive to remain clean in his eyes.

17 What happens to the sins of those whom God favors? As noted earlier, Jehovah said through Jeremiah: "I shall forgive their error, and their sin I shall remember no more." (Jer. 31:34) God does this for the anointed on the basis of Jesus' sacrifice. In a similar way, God can forgive the sins of the great crowd on the basis of the same "blood of the covenant." Jeremiah's saying that

---

16. What encouragement can the "great crowd" gain from Revelation 7:9, 14?
17. In what sense does Jehovah "remember" sins no more?

## You Can Benefit From the New Covenant

God would "remember" sins no more does not imply that He would have a memory lapse and simply not be able to recall the sins. Rather, it indicates that once Jehovah has administered any needed discipline and forgiven a repentant sinner, God throws that past sin behind Him. Think of the sins King David committed involving Bath-sheba and Uriah. David received discipline and felt the consequences of his sins. (2 Sam. 11:4, 15, 27; 12:9-14; Isa. 38:17) Yet, God did not keep holding David accountable for those sins. (*Read 2 Chronicles 7:17, 18.*) As indicated in the new covenant, once Jehovah has forgiven sins, based on Jesus' sacrifice, He remembers them no more.—Ezek. 18:21, 22.

¹⁸ Accordingly, the new covenant highlights a wonderful aspect of Jehovah's dealings with sinful humans, both the anointed, who are in the covenant, and those with an earthly hope. You can trust that once Jehovah has dealt with your sins, he will not bring them up again. God's promise about the new covenant thus offers a lesson for each of us. Ask yourself, 'Do I try to imitate Jehovah by not dredging up the offenses of others, errors that I have already said I forgave?' (Matt. 6:14, 15) This applies to small offenses as well as to very serious ones, such as a Christian mate's sin of adultery. If the innocent one agrees to forgive the repentant adulterer, is it not right to 'remember the sin no more'? Granted, our putting errors behind us may not be easy, yet it is one way that we can imitate Jehovah.\*

---

\* God's willingness to forgive was illustrated in Hosea's course toward Gomer. See the comments on Hosea 2:14-16 in *Live With Jehovah's Day in Mind*, pages 128-130.

18, 19. The new covenant contains what lesson about forgiveness?

¹⁹ We can apply this lesson related to the new covenant even as respects someone who was disfellowshipped but repented and was reinstated. What if that person had caused you loss or had defamed you in some way? Now he is accepted back into the congregation. How will what we read at Jeremiah 31:34 influence our personal thinking and response? Will we forgive the transgressor and not keep bringing up the wrong again? (2 Cor. 2:6-8) Truly, that is something that all who appreciate the new covenant should try to apply in real life.

*How can you apply a lesson about forgiveness illustrated in the new covenant?*

## PRESENT AND FUTURE BLESSINGS OF THE NEW COVENANT

²⁰ In Jeremiah's day, many Jews were saying, in effect: "Jehovah will not do good, and he will not do bad." (Zeph. 1:12) Although they had some knowledge of who Jehovah is and what he is like, they felt that he would not take action; nor would he expect them to live up to any standards. You, though, know that nothing escapes divine attention. You have a respectful fear of God and definitely want to refrain from doing bad. (Jer. 16:17) At the same time, you know Jehovah to be a benevolent Father. He takes note of our good deeds, whether others see them or not.—2 Chron. 16:9.

²¹ A significant aspect of the new covenant is this: "I will put my law within them, and in their heart I shall

---

20. How is your attitude different from that of many in Jeremiah's day?
21, 22. Why do you no longer need to be told: "Know Jehovah"?

You Can Benefit From the New Covenant 179

**Those who have served God faithfully will enjoy his future blessings**

write it. And I will become their God, . . . And they will no more teach each one his companion and each one his brother, saying, 'Know Jehovah!' for they will all of them know me." (Jer. 31:33, 34) The anointed on earth today have shown that they have God's law within them. They love the truths found in it, rather than relying on the teachings of any human. And they have happily shared Bible knowledge with those forming the great crowd. Thus, these with an earthly hope have also come to know and love Jehovah. They willingly submit to his direction and trust in his promises. You probably fit that description. You know him as a Person and have a personal relationship with him. What a benefit that is!

²² How have you been able to strengthen your relationship with Jehovah? You no doubt remember occasions when you felt that he answered your prayers. Through such experiences, you deepened your appreciation for the kind of God he is. You may have sensed his assistance as you recalled a scripture that helped you to cope with adversity. Cherish such experiences. As you keep on studying his Word, your knowledge of him will continue to increase—an ongoing benefit.

²³ But linked to the new covenant is another blessing that we can experience now. Knowing Jehovah as the one who provides forgiveness in line with that covenant can help free us of persistent feelings of guilt. For example, some who had an abortion before they knew God's standard may sense guilt and sadness because they deliberately ended the life of a developing human. Others feel that way because they took lives when they engaged in warfare. Jesus' ransom sacrifice—fundamental to the new covenant—provides for forgiveness of truly repentant ones. That being so, should we not be convinced that if Jehovah has forgiven our sins, he views the matter as closed? We need not dwell on the sins that Jehovah has bountifully forgiven.

---

23. How can knowing Jehovah free you from unnecessary troubling feelings?

## You Can Benefit From the New Covenant

<sup>24</sup> We find graphic evidence of God's forgiveness at Jeremiah 31:20. (*Read.*) Decades before Jeremiah's day, Jehovah punished the ten-tribe northern kingdom of Israel (represented by Ephraim, the prominent tribe) because of their idolatry. They were taken into exile. Yet, God was deeply attached to the people of that nation and showed them tender affection. He still cherished them as "a fondly treated child." When he thought about them, his intestines 'became boisterous,' meaning that his deep feelings were touched. This account, found in the context of the new covenant, shows how largehearted Jehovah is toward those who repent of past misconduct.

<sup>25</sup> Jehovah's promise to forgive sins through the new covenant will reach its fullest extent at the end of Christ's Millennial Reign. Jesus Christ, together with the 144,000 underpriests, will have restored to perfection loyal humans. After the final test, mankind will then be full-fledged members of Jehovah's universal family. (*Read Romans 8:19-22.*) For centuries, all have been groaning under the burden of sin. However, Jehovah's human creation will then have "the glorious freedom of the children of God," freedom from sin and death. Consequently, be confident that through the loving arrangement of the new covenant, you can obtain abundant benefits. You can benefit now and forever through the "sprout" for David and enjoy "righteousness in the land."—Jer. 33:15.

---

24. What encouragement can you draw from the account at Jeremiah 31:20?
25. Why can you be grateful to Jehovah for the new covenant?

***How can you benefit from the new covenant now and in the future?***

## Chapter Fifteen

# "I Cannot Keep Silent"

"HEAR the word of Jehovah." Those words rang in the streets and squares of Jerusalem starting in 647 B.C.E. And God's prophet did not let up. Even when the city was destroyed 40 years later, he repeated that exhortation. (Jer. 2:4; 42:15) Almighty God sent prophets to make sure that the Jews could hear His counsel and repent. As shown earlier in this volume, Jeremiah was outstanding among those divine spokesmen. When commissioning him, God told Jeremiah: "You must rise up and speak to them everything that I myself command you. Do not be struck with any terror." (Jer. 1:17) The work was demanding. Jeremiah suffered physical and emotional pain, but despite such trials, he was impelled to fulfill his assignment. He said: "My heart is boisterous within me. I cannot keep silent."—Jer. 4:19.

² The way Jeremiah carried out his prophetic assignment set an example for future servants of Jehovah. (Jas. 5:10) Shortly after Pentecost 33 C.E., the Jewish authorities arrested the apostles Peter and John, ordering them to stop preaching. You have read their response. "We cannot stop speaking about the things we have seen and heard." (Acts 4:19, 20) After threatening to do worse to

---

1. Why did Jeremiah and other prophets of Jehovah not keep silent?
2, 3. (a) How did Jesus' disciples imitate Jeremiah? (b) Why should you follow Jeremiah's example?

them the next time, the rulers let Peter and John go. You know the result. Those faithful men would not and did not stop preaching.

³ Can you see how the words of Peter and John recorded at Acts 4:20 echo Jeremiah's fervor? As a minister of Jehovah God in these decisive last days, are you not just as determined in thinking, 'I cannot remain silent!' Let us see how we can maintain strength like that of Jeremiah to continue preaching the good news despite worsening conditions around us.

## CONTINUE DESPITE APATHY

⁴ Are you not confident that God's promise of a wonderful future under his Son's rule is the best news that people can hear? Yet, many today express themselves as some Jews once did by saying to Jeremiah: "As regards the word that you have spoken to us in the name of Jehovah, we are not listening to you." (Jer. 29:19; 44:16) Jeremiah often heard such sentiments. So do Jehovah's servants today, for many people say, "I am not interested." Widespread apathy could sap the zeal of Kingdom publishers. If that has been true in your territory, among some in your congregation, or even in your case, what can be done?

⁵ Consider the thinking that Jeremiah developed in the face of the largely apathetic people of Judah. Early in Jeremiah's career, Jehovah gave him a foreview of the coming divine judgment. (*Read Jeremiah 4:23-26.*) The prophet could then see that the lives of thousands

---

4. What attitude was common in ancient Jerusalem?
5. (a) How did Jeremiah react to the people's apathy? (b) Why are those who are apathetic toward the good news in grave danger?

## APATHY CAN TURN INTO INTEREST

A householder in New Zealand said that she had never listened to the Witnesses before, but now she was interested. That week she had attended the funeral of a Witness because her husband worked secularly with the deceased sister's husband. The woman noted that many present gave personal comfort to the grieving widower. Also, she said that the clear Biblical explanation of our resurrection hope made sense.

The woman explained that she trained hospice nurses, who care for the terminally ill. As a result of the funeral, she had encouraged her students to attend a funeral conducted by Jehovah's Witnesses. Why? She remarked to the Witnesses at her door that she told her students that the Witnesses explain the true condition of the dead and offer a beautiful hope for the future. She felt that the nurses could use both points to encourage their patients.

Clearly, the fact that people have long been apathetic does not mean that Jehovah cannot 'give them a heart to know him.' (Jer. 24:7) Those who have been apathetic in your territory may yet respond.

depended on their hearing the words he would speak and acting on them. Today, people are in a similar situation, including those in your territory. Regarding "that day" of God's judgment against today's wicked world, Jesus said: "It will come in upon all those dwelling upon the face of all the earth. Keep awake, then, all the time making supplication that you may succeed in escaping all these things that are destined to occur, and in standing before the Son of man." (Luke 21:34-36) You can conclude from Jesus' words that those who reject the good news are in grave danger.

⁶ However, those who shake off indifference and who listen and respond to Jehovah's word that we present will receive priceless benefits. God is opening the way for us to escape destruction and enter into his new world. In some respects, it was similar in Jeremiah's ministry. The inhabitants of Judah could escape. (*Read Jeremiah 26:2, 3.*) To help them, Jeremiah spent decades urging the people to "listen and return," to heed the word of the true God. We do not know how many repented and changed their lives as a result of the prophet's witnessing. But some did, and so have many in our time. As we continue to preach the good news, we often hear about how hearts of once unresponsive people soften. (See the box "Apathy Can Turn Into Interest," on page 184.) Is that not an added reason to stay active in our lifesaving ministry of the good news?

---

6. Why should you keep preaching, even to those who show little interest in your message?

*Why are you determined to preach the good news despite any apathy you face?*

## OPPOSERS CAN DO NO LASTING HARM

⁷ One remarkable aspect of Jeremiah's ministry is how frequently opposers tried to destroy him and his work. False prophets contradicted him in public. (Jer. 14:13-16) As Jeremiah walked the streets of Jerusalem, bystanders shouted abuse, deriding him. (Jer. 15:10) Some of his enemies plotted additional ways to discredit him. (Jer. 18:18) Others carried out an intense whispering campaign to turn honesthearted ones away from the divine truths Jeremiah was preaching. (Lam. 3:61, 62) Did Jeremiah give up? On the contrary, he kept on preaching. How did he do it?

⁸ Jeremiah's main weapon in battling all the opposition was trust in Jehovah. At the beginning of Jeremiah's ministry, God told him that He would sustain and protect him. (*Read Jeremiah 1:18, 19.*) Jeremiah put faith in that promise, and Jehovah did not let him down. As opposers applied pressure and tried more drastic measures, he grew in boldness, valor, and endurance. Notice how those qualities served him well.

⁹ On one occasion, rebellious priests and prophets hauled Jeremiah before the princes of Judah to have him put to death. Did their threats frighten Jeremiah into inaction? No. His response disproved the charges of those apostates so effectively that his life was spared.—*Read Jeremiah 26:11-16;* Luke 21:12-15.

¹⁰ Recall that after listening to the prophet's powerful message, a temple official named Pashhur put him

---

7. How did enemies attempt to destroy Jeremiah's prophetic work?
8. As opposers increased their efforts against him, how did Jeremiah respond?
9, 10. What incidents in Jeremiah's life should encourage you to be bold?

*"I Cannot Keep Silent"* 187

in stocks. Pashhur must have concluded that this would teach Jeremiah a lesson and that he would now keep quiet. So the next day, Pashhur let him go. But Jeremiah, certainly very sore because of the torment he had experienced, spoke directly to Pashhur, declaring Jehovah's judgment against him. No, even torture did not silence Jeremiah! (Jer. 20:1-6) Why not? Jeremiah himself tells us: "Jehovah was with me like a terrible mighty one. That is why the very ones persecuting me will stumble and not prevail." (Jer. 20:11) Even when confronted by fierce opposers, Jeremiah did not cower. His trust in Jehovah was well-founded, and yours can be too.

¹¹ It is good to bear in mind that Jeremiah was not a fanatic. He used common sense when facing opposers. He knew when to withdraw. For instance, consider his experience with Hananiah. After that false prophet contradicted Jehovah's prophetic word in public, Jeremiah corrected him and explained how to recognize a true

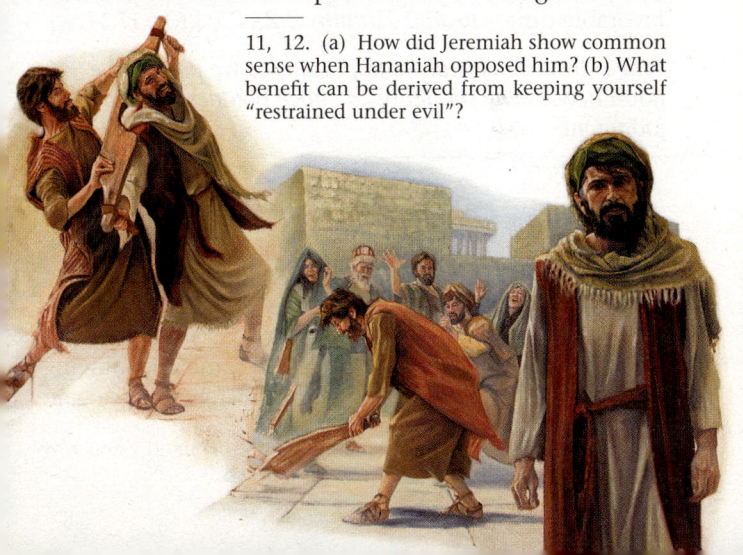

---

11, 12. (a) How did Jeremiah show common sense when Hananiah opposed him? (b) What benefit can be derived from keeping yourself "restrained under evil"?

prophet. Jeremiah had been carrying a wooden yoke to signify coming under the yoke of Babylon; Hananiah got violent and broke the yoke. Who could know what Hananiah would do next? So, what did Jeremiah do? We read: "The prophet proceeded to go his way." Yes, Jeremiah left the scene. Later, at Jehovah's direction, he returned and told Hananiah what God would bring about —bondage to the king of Babylon for the Jews and death for Hananiah.—Jer. 28:1-17.

[12] It is clear from this inspired account that in preaching, we do well to couple our boldness with sound judgment. If at one home someone refuses to accept Scriptural reasoning and becomes angry, even threatening violence, we can excuse ourselves courteously and move on to another house. There is no need to have a heated argument with anyone regarding the good news of the Kingdom. By keeping ourselves "restrained under evil," we leave the way open to help the householder at a more favorable time.—*Read 2 Timothy 2:23-25;* Prov. 17:14.

*Why is trust in Jehovah so important as we preach the good news? Why should we balance boldness with good judgment?*

## "DO NOT BE AFRAID"

[13] True worshippers were affected by the appalling conditions that prevailed before Jerusalem's destruction in 607 B.C.E. You can thus understand why God told Jeremiah: "Do not be afraid." (Jer. 1:8; Lam. 3:57) And Jehovah had him tell others of his people the same encouraging words. (*Read Jeremiah 46:27.*) What insight can we gain

---

13. Why did Jehovah tell Jeremiah: "Do not be afraid," and why should we consider this?

*"I Cannot Keep Silent"*

from this? In this dangerous time of the end, we could occasionally feel fear. At such times, will we listen to Jehovah, who in effect is telling us: "Do not be afraid"? Earlier in this volume, we considered how God sustained Jeremiah during that truly fearful time. Let us briefly review what happened, in order to see a lesson in it for us.

¹⁴ As the Babylonians tightened their grip on Jerusalem, hunger overtook the people. Soon many were without food. (Jer. 37:21) As if the famine were not enough, Jeremiah was trapped in a place that could become his grave. The princes of Judah had pressed weak-willed King Zedekiah to acquiesce. Then they had Jeremiah thrown into a deep cistern. There was no water in it, just a lot of mire. As Jeremiah began sinking into the mud, he could see no human way out. If you had been in that situation, would you not have felt some fear?—Jer. 38:4-6.

¹⁵ Though he was a mortal like us, Jeremiah trusted Jehovah's word that He would never abandon him. (*Read Jeremiah 15:20, 21.*) Did Jehovah reward that trust? We know for a fact that he did. God moved Ebed-melech to defy the princes and rescue Jeremiah. With the king's permission, Ebed-melech pulled the prophet up out of the cistern, rescuing him from death in that muddy deep.—Jer. 38:7-13.

¹⁶ Even when Jeremiah was back standing on solid ground, he was not out of danger. Pleading in Jeremiah's behalf, Ebed-melech had told the king: "He will die where he is because of the famine. For there is no bread anymore in the city." (Jer. 38:9) Food was so scarce in Jerusalem that people were resorting to cannibalism.

---

14, 15. (a) In what dangerous situation did Jeremiah find himself?
(b) How did Jehovah fulfill his promise to protect Jeremiah?
16. From what dangers did Jehovah rescue his loyal ones?

Yet, Jehovah again intervened to save his prophet. And Jeremiah passed on to Ebed-melech a guarantee of protection from Jehovah. (Jer. 39:16-18) Jeremiah had not forgotten God's assurance: "I am with you to deliver you." (Jer. 1:8) With Almighty God guarding those two loyal men, neither human enemies nor hunger would finish them off. They escaped death in that doomed city. What is the point? Jehovah promised protection and fulfilled his promise.—Jer. 40:1-4.

¹⁷ The fulfillment of Jesus' prophecy about the conclusion of the system of things is moving inexorably toward its climax. In the near future, there will occur "signs in sun and moon and stars, and on the earth anguish of nations, not knowing the way out . . . while men become faint out of fear and expectation of the things coming upon the inhabited earth." (Luke 21:25, 26) We must wait to see what form those signs will take and what terror they produce among many. No matter what develops, though, you need never doubt Jehovah's ability and desire to save his people. The out-

---

17. Why should you put faith in Jehovah's promise to protect his servants?

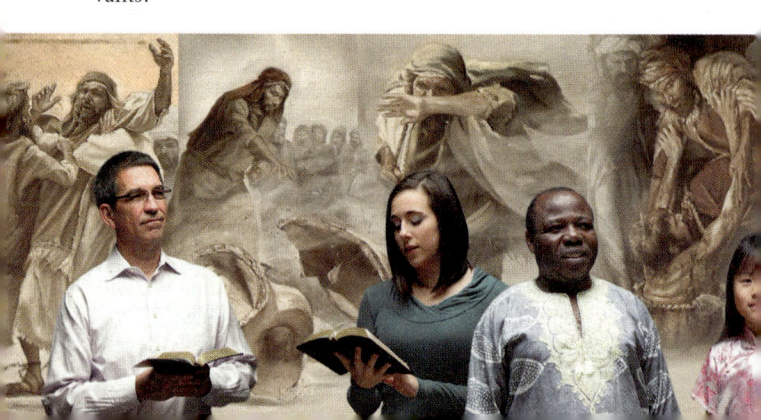

*"I Cannot Keep Silent"*

come for those who do not have his favor, however, will be quite different. (*Read Jeremiah 8:20; 14:9.*) Even if it seems that his servants are in a condition as hopeless as the dank, dark bottom of a cistern, he can rescue them! God's words to Ebed-melech will apply to his people: " 'I shall without fail furnish you an escape, and by the sword you will not fall; and you will certainly come to have your soul as a spoil, because you have trusted in me,' is the utterance of Jehovah."—Jer. 39:18.

## WORDS WRITTEN FOR YOU

[18] "To all those to whom I shall send you, you should go; and everything that I shall command you, you should speak." (Jer. 1:7) Jeremiah's life changed forever when he heard that command from God. From that moment forward, his overwhelming concern was to announce "the word of Jehovah." That phrase appears repeatedly throughout the book of Jeremiah. In the last chapter, Jeremiah relates the capture of Jerusalem and the exiling of its last king, Zedekiah. Yes, Jeremiah continued teaching and exhorting the people of Judah to obey Jehovah until events made it clear that his work was complete.

[19] There are many parallels between Jeremiah's assignment and the public ministry of Jehovah's Witnesses today. Like him, you serve the true God during a time of judgment. Other responsibilities require some of your time and energy; yet the preaching of the good news

---

18. (a) What words changed Jeremiah's life? (b) What meaning does God's command at Jeremiah 1:7 have for you?
19, 20. (a) Why is Jeremiah's service a pattern for you? (b) What link is there between the preaching work and finding joy and contentment? (c) How has considering the books of Jeremiah and Lamentations affected you?

is by far the most significant work you can do in this system of things. By means of it, you exalt God's great name and accept his absolute right and authority as Universal Sovereign. (*Read Lamentations 5:19.*) You also demonstrate outstanding love for neighbor by helping others to know the true God and his requirements for life.—Jer. 25:3-6.

[20] Regarding the work that Jehovah gave him to do, Jeremiah said: "Your word becomes to me the exultation and the rejoicing of my heart; for your name has been called upon me, O Jehovah God of armies." (Jer. 15:16) Such rejoicing and contentment are set before all today whose hearts move them to speak on behalf of the true God. You thus have good reason to keep proclaiming Jehovah's message, as did Jeremiah.

*How can the examples of Jeremiah and Ebed-melech help you to be courageous? What quality of Jeremiah do you want to imitate as you preach?*

---

**SELECTED OFFICES OF JEHOVAH'S WITNESSES**

**AUSTRALIA:** PO Box 280, Ingleburn, NSW 1890. **BAHAMAS:** PO Box N-1247, Nassau, NP. **BARBADOS, W.I.:** Crusher Site Road, Prospect, BB 24012 St. James. **BRITAIN:** The Ridgeway, London NW7 1RN. **CAMEROON:** BP 889, Douala. **CANADA:** PO Box 4100, Georgetown, ON L7G 4Y4. **CURAÇAO, NETHERLANDS ANTILLES:** PO Box 4708, Willemstad. **FRANCE:** BP 625, F-27406 Louviers cedex. **GERMANY:** Am Steinfels, 65618 Selters. **GHANA:** PO Box GP 760, Accra. **GUYANA:** 352-360 Tyrell St, Republic Park Phase 2 EBD. **HAWAII:** 2055 Kamehameha IV Road, Honolulu, HI 96819-2619. **HONG KONG:** 4 Kent Road, Kowloon Tong, Kowloon. **INDIA:** PO Box 6441, Yelahanka, Bangalore-KAR 560 064. **IRELAND:** Newcastle, Greystones, Co. Wicklow. **ITALY:** Via della Bufalotta 1281, I-00138 Rome RM. **JAMAICA:** PO Box 103, Old Harbour, St. Catherine. **JAPAN:** 4-7-1 Nakashinden, Ebina City, Kanagawa-Pref, 243-0496. **KENYA:** PO Box 21290, Nairobi 00505. **LIBERIA:** PO Box 10-0380, 1000 Monrovia 10. **MEXICO:** Apartado Postal 895, 06002 Mexico, DF. **NEW ZEALAND:** PO Box 75142, Manurewa, Manukau 2243. **NIGERIA:** PMB 1090, Benin City 300001, Edo State. **PHILIPPINES:** PO Box 2044, 1060 Manila. **PUERTO RICO:** PO Box 3980, Guaynabo, PR 00970. **SOUTH AFRICA:** Private Bag X2067, Krugersdorp, 1740. **SPAIN:** Apartado 132, 28850 Torrejón de Ardoz (Madrid). **TRINIDAD AND TOBAGO:** Lower Rapsey Street & Laxmi Lane, Curepe. **UGANDA:** PO Box 4019, Kampala. **UNITED STATES OF AMERICA:** 25 Columbia Heights, Brooklyn, NY 11201-2483. **ZAMBIA:** PO Box 33459, 10101 Lusaka. www.watchtower.org